It's a Shore Thing...

Culinary Favorites from Chicago's North Shore

Junior League of Evanston-North Shore

Evanston Lighthouse

JUNIOR LEAGUE OF EVANSTON-NORTH SHORE

Women building better communities

- JLE-NS MISSION STATEMENT -

Junior League of Evanston-North Shore, Inc. is
an organization of women committed to promoting voluntarism,
developing the potential of women and improving communities through
the effective action and leadership of trained volunteers.

The Junior League of Evanston-North Shore's
purpose is exclusively educational and charitable.

First Printing, March 2006

Copyright © 2006
All rights reserved

ISBN 0-9785080-0-9

Cover photograph by Dave Norehad Photography
Various town/village illustrations by Gail Elaine Harwood
Map illustration by Julie Child

WIMMER
COOKBOOKS

A CONSOLIDATED GRAPHICS COMPANY

800.548.2537   wimmerco.com

Foreword
- BY ART SMITH -

I love the Chicago area! Having traveled all over the world, I must say there really is no place like home. The diverse city neighborhoods and suburbs have so much to offer from a cultural, educational, architectural, entertainment and, of course, culinary perspective.

Chicago's North Shore is one of our city's finest gems and you do not have to live there to appreciate it. A journey up Lake Shore Drive along the Lake Michigan shoreline to Sheridan Road offers a blissful visual prelude to the area. The tree-lined streets, with their Old English-style lamp posts and stately century-old homes, extend a warm welcome to visitors.

Much like the recipes in this book, the North Shore boasts some of the regions finest ingredients. Food and entertaining enthusiasts have long appreciated the many outstanding purveyors available in the area, including an assortment of:

- Country-style Farmers' Markets
- European-style Grocers
- Fine Neighborhood Meat Markets
- Fresh Seafood Markets
- Old town Bakeries
- Eclectic Wine Shops
- World Class Chocolatiers

When mixed together and infused with a century of hospitality and splendid history, the area becomes a destination for both people who like to cook and those who love to eat.

This cookbook features a lovely culmination of recipes, cooking tips and entertainment ideas designed to enhance every occasion from basic beachside barbeques to elegant cocktail affairs. The Junior League of Evanston-North Shore has done a fantastic job of serving up a taste of the North Shore while providing a flavor of the communities that make up its rich history. Here's to celebrating the people, food and culture of the North Shore with this wonderful new cookbook!

Bon Apetit!
Art Smith, Personal Chef to Oprah Winfrey
and Best Selling Author

It is with much gratitude that we thank the following
Corporate Sponsors for their financial support...

- PLATINUM SPONSORS -
North Shore Community Bank and Trust
The Grand Food Center

- SILVER SPONSOR -
Nielsen-Massey Vanillas, Inc.

- BRONZE SPONSOR -
Foodstuffs Gourmet Foods & Catering

It is with much gratitude that we thank
the following individuals for their financial support...

- PLATINUM SPONSORS -
Rebecca and Victor Garces
Theresa Gernand
Karen and Tim Miller
Beth and Doug Mikel
Helen and Ray Quick

- SILVER SPONSORS -
Marley and Tim Crane
Amy and Cameron Findlay
Alissa and Philip Preston
Michele Dunard (JLE-NS Founder's Award Recipient 2001)

- BRONZE SPONSORS -

Mary Arden M. Bretland
Heather and William Burgess
Kathy and Jeff Cullerton
Maria and Bruce Doughty
Nancy and Brian D. Free
Kathie and Peter Hamilton
Molly and David Jarmusz

Michele and Andrew Kaufman
Jane and Gerald Lahey
Susan and Bryan Locke
Julie and Bradley Simmons
Kathryn and Jon Talty
Pia and Jim Thompson
Mary M. Walther

Introduction

We are so excited to share this cookbook with you! We live in a beautiful part of the country. We have all four seasons of the year. Many of our communities border beautiful Lake Michigan. We are a community of residents that has been around for generations, as well as more recent additions from all over the country and the world - a virtual melting pot. This combination has lent itself very well to collecting a lively variety of recipes to share.

A Shore Thing: Culinary Favorites from Chicago's North Shore, at the highest level, is not only a collection of recipes, but also a collection of community histories. It is only appropriate therefore to provide a brief history of the dedicated and fun organization that brings you this book...

Our League's story starts in 1923 after Dorothy Mason, our first League President, and Frances Charles visited friends that were Junior League members in New York. On the train journey back to the Midwest, they decided they would start in earnest to assemble a Junior League in Evanston. The Junior Leagues of Chicago and Montclair (now Montclair-Newark) sponsored the admission of our 27 member League into the Association of Junior Leagues in 1924.

Since then the Junior League of Evanston-North Shore has been successful at addressing community needs through many outreach projects. In our League's 80-plus year history, we have done well in various media: producing a number of radio programs, producing a video on grief that was aired on television and publishing a book, *An Architectural Album of the North Shore.* We had yet to accomplish the traditional "Junior League Cookbook".

It was our intent that this cookbook highlight the richness of our history, as well as the breadth of culture and diversity in the community that is Chicago's North Shore. The time has been right to bring together this collection of recipes from, not only our League members, but also our community leaders, celebrities, businesses, notable chefs and significant restaurants. Admittedly, this cookbook is also a means to an end - to raise funds for the improvement of our community. We appreciate your support in this endeavor. It is with much pride that we present to you this window to our community and our kitchens.

As my father would say..."Enjoy!"
Rebecca M. Garces
Cookbook Chair 2004-2005
JLE-NS President-Elect 2004-2005
Junior League of Evanston-North Shore President 2005-2006

2004-2005 Cookbook Committee

Cookbook Chair - Rebecca Garces

Theresa Gernand, Alissa Preston, Elizabeth Thomas, Ann Diaz, Karen Miller,
Karen Cosgrove, Deborah Gale, Laura Henderson, Jenny McGlinn,
Leesa Ullerich, Michele Dunard, Amy Findlay, Shavaun Adams Taylor

2005-2006 Cookbook Committee

Cookbook Co-Chairs - Amy Maher, Alissa Preston, Elizabeth Thomas

Rebecca Garces, Theresa Gernand, Ann Diaz, Kelly Kraklau Bosker,
Beth Kauffman, Nell Pike, Nicole Bogdanovich, Pia Thompson, Nancy Free,
Rita Brogley and Beth Mikel (Fundraising Treasurer)

Thank you to the following Historical Societies for help with our research:
Evanston Historical Society
Glencoe Historical Society
Glenview Historical Society
Highland Park Historical Society
Kenilworth Historical Society
Lake Forest Historical Society
Northfield Historical Society
Wilmette Historical Society
Winnetka Historical Society

Community Partners

Mr. Tolbert Chisum (Community Volunteer Award Recipient 1998 and 2005)
Chicago's North Shore Convention and Visitor's Bureau

Celebrity Recipe Contributors

Art Smith

Barbara Bush

Barbara Rinella

Bill Carmody, Head Basketball Coach
    at Northwestern University, Evanston

Chris and Kate Kennedy

Emery and Aaron Moorehead

Lady Margaret Thatcher

Lili Taylor

Liz Phair

Murray Brothers
    (Bill, Andy, Ed, Brian, John and Joel)

Scott Turow

Virginia Madsen

Noteworthy Recipe Contibutors

Marian Baird, JLE-NS President 1955-1957
Beverly Dawson - Past President of the Glenview Historical Society
Christopher S. Canning - Village of Wilmette President
Ed Woodbury - Village of Winnetka
Glencoe Public Safety
Jan Schakowsky - Illinois Congresswoman
Jan-Roman Potocki, Potocki Vodka
John L. Birkinbine, Jr. - President of the Village of Northfield
Kathy Taslitz Interiors
Lori Andre - Lori's Designer Shoes
Lorraine Morton - Mayor of Evanston
Michael Belsky - Mayor of Highland Park
Mike Rummel - Mayor of Lake Forest
Nielsen-Massey Vanillas, Inc
Old Willow Wine Shoppe
Paul Shafer - Chief of Police - Highland Park Police Department
Rizvana Adanjee, JLE-NS Scholarship Recipient
Roberta Rubin, The Bookstall
Scott Feldman, President of the Village of Glencoe
Tolbert Chisum - President of the Village of Kenilworth
Walter E. Smithe Custom Furniture
Winnetka Historical Society

Chef/Restaurant Recipe Contributors

Burhop's Seafood, Wilmette

Charles Murray, Cajun Charlie's
New Orleans Kitchen, Evanston

Betsy Simson, Corner Cooks, Winnetka

Dave's Italian Kitchen, Evanston

Chef Jeffrey Tomchek, Deer Path Inn,
Lake Forest

Depot Restaurant, Winnetka

David Jones, Food2U Catering

Grand Food Centers, Winnetka and
Glencoe

Chef Jim Lovell, Lovells, Lake Forest

Metropolitan Café, Highland Park

Metropolitan Club, Chicago

Chef Mark Grosz, Oceanique, Evanston

Song O'Sixpence, Winnetka

Sweet Baby Ray's

Chef Victor Hernandez, The Stained
Glass Restaurant, Evanston

Three Tarts Bakery and Catering, Northfield

Contents

Breakfast & Breads

Charles Gates Dawes House

- Evanston -

Evanston

The major landmark for the city of Evanston, Northwestern University, was actually founded before the city itself in 1851. The first classes were held with four students and taught by Henry S. Noyes and William Goodman. In 1854, the founders of the university, including John Evans, submitted their plans to the country judge for a city and changed the existing town from Ridgeville to Evanston.

Nationally recognized as one of the country's leading academic institutions, Northwestern University is home to the Feinberg School of Medicine, Kellogg School of Management and Medill School of Journalism. Many of our cultural leaders got their start at Northwestern, including Charlton Heston, Ann Margret, Sidney Sheldon and David Sanborn.

The charming college town on Lake Michigan continued to grow with the help of the citizen's ingenuity. Known for its architecture and beautiful homes on the lakefront, it is also known as the birthplace of Tinker Toys, automobile racing, and, as legend has it, the ice cream sundae.

Charles Dawes, the Vice President of the United States under Calvin Coolege, lived in Evanston until his death in 1951. His stately home is now the site of the Evanston Historical Society. It was the home of our League from 1961 to 1992.

Community spirit and civic duty is a passion in Evanston. There are numerous not-for profit organizations located here: Rotary International Headquarters, The League of Women Voters, YWCA, and the Junior League of Evanston were founded here in 1924.

With the many cultural outlets, thriving business economy and public lakefront recreation activities, Evanston continues to prosper.

Sunday Football Party

Kick off Northwestern's Wildcats season with this winning menu.

Buffalo Chicken Dip

Oriental Ribs

Tailgate Sausage Bread

White Bean Chicken Chili

All Year Round Cobbler

Lorraine's Down-Home Breakfast

Contributed by Lorraine H. Morton, Mayor of Evanston.

1 center slice of country ham
brown sugar to taste

⅓ cup coffee
prepared grits

Soak ham in warm water for 30 minutes. Dry on paper towel. Trim fat from outer edges. Pan-fry edges over low temperature until oil is produced. Remove edges. If not enough oil, add vegetable oil. Add ham slice and cook on medium 5 minutes. Flip ham and cook 5 minutes more. Sprinkle brown sugar over ham. Pour coffee or water over the ham, cover and simmer about 3 minutes. This makes Red Eye Gravy. Pour gravy over grits. Serve with scrambled eggs, apples (Granny Smith apples) fried in butter, biscuits and butter.

Yield: 4 servings

À la Lorraine Scrambled Eggs

Contributed by Lorraine H. Morton, Mayor of Evanston.

eggs
½ teaspoon water per egg
dash of salt

¼ teaspoon vanilla according to number of eggs, do not exceed 1 teaspoon
sugar to taste
dash of Tabasco sauce

Break eggs into a bowl. Add water, salt, vanilla, sugar and Tabasco. Whisk until blended. Cook in a greased hot skillet.

Yield: Calories galore!

Low-Fat, High-Protein, Zone-Style Breakfast Omelet

Contributed by Scott Turow.

Mr. Turow is an international best-selling author who resides in the North Shore. His works include Presumed Innocent, Reversible Errors, *and* The Burden of Proof *along with his newest novel,* Ordinary Heroes.

1 (4-ounce) carton egg substitute
broccoli florets
mushrooms, sliced

green onions, chopped
3 slices Canadian bacon, chopped

Heat a non-stick skillet over medium heat. Pour in egg substitute. Top with broccoli, mushrooms, onions and bacon. Cook egg. Flip the omelet and cook the other side. Slide omelet onto plate.

Yield: 1 serving

Quiche Lorraine

Contributed by Grand Food Centers, Winnetka and Glencoe.

1 (9-inch) frozen or refrigerated pie crust

½ cup shredded Swiss cheese

¼ cup diced ham

¼ cup diced cooked bacon

3 green onions, sliced

5 eggs

1 pint half-and-half

1 pint whole milk

1 teaspoon salt

1 teaspoon pepper

pinch freshly ground nutmeg

parsley sprigs for garnish

Pierce the bottom of the pie crust several times with a fork. Bake at 350 degrees 5 minutes or until crust is slightly firm. Use pie weights if you have them so that the crust does not puff. Cool slightly. Sprinkle cheese, ham, bacon and onions evenly over the bottom. Beat together the eggs, half-and-half, milk, salt, pepper and nutmeg. Pour into the crust. Bake for 45 minutes or until set. Cool before slicing and garnish with parsley.

Yield: 8 servings

Ginger Bread

Contributed by Song O· Sixpence Specialty Foods and Catering, Winnetka.

This is a great bread for breakfast or dessert;
spicy and rich and incredibly moist. Full of flavor!!!

7 cups all-purpose flour

2 tablespoons baking powder

1 teaspoon baking soda

1 teaspoon salt

2 teaspoons ground ginger

2 teaspoons ground cloves

2 teaspoons dry mustard

2 teaspoons pepper

1½ cups butter, softened

3 cups packed light brown sugar

6 eggs

3 cups molasses

2 cups very strong decaf coffee

Combine flour, baking powder, baking soda, salt, ginger, cloves, mustard and pepper. Set aside. Cream butter and sugar. Add eggs, one at a time. Slowly add molasses in a steady stream. Stir in coffee. Add dry ingredients until just incorporated. Pour batter into buttered, floured bread or cake pans. Bake at 375 degrees 30 to 40 minutes.
For cake pans, bake 20 to 30 minutes.

Yield: 3 large loaves

Zucchini Carrot Muffins

Contributed by Three Tarts Bakery & Café, Northfield.

We suggest that all ingredients be measured and at
room temperature before proceeding with mixing.

2 cups all-purpose flour	1/4 teaspoon ground allspice
1/2 teaspoon salt	2 eggs
1/2 teaspoon baking soda	1 cup granulated sugar
3/4 teaspoon baking powder	1/2 cup canola oil
1 1/2 teaspoons cinnamon	1 1/4 teaspoons vanilla
1/4 teaspoon ground ginger	1 cup of grated zucchini
1/8 teaspoon ground cloves	1 cup of grated carrots

Preheat oven to 375 degrees. Adjust rack to center of oven. Combine flour, salt, baking soda, baking powder, cinnamon, ginger, cloves and allspice. Using a 5 quart mixer with paddle attachment, blend eggs and sugar until thickened. Beat in oil and vanilla. Reduce speed to stir and mix in zucchini and carrots. Reduce speed and add dry ingredients. Continue mixing just until combined. Scrape bowl and mix a few seconds more. Do not over mix. Remove bowl from mixer. Spoon batter into paper-lined muffin cups filling three-fourths full. Bake 15 minutes. Turn pan 180 degrees and bake 8 minutes more or until toothpick comes out clean. Remove from pan and cool on a rack. Store in air-tight container.

Yield: Baker's Dozen (13)

Gail's Sour Cream Coffee Cake

Contributed by Song O' Sixpence Specialty Foods and Catering, Winnetka.

½ cup butter, softened

1 cup sugar

2 eggs

2 cups all-purpose flour

1½ teaspoons baking powder

1 cup sour cream

1 teaspoon baking soda

1 teaspoon vanilla

½ cup packed brown sugar

½ cup chopped pecans

2 teaspoons cinnamon

powdered sugar

Cream butter and sugar until light and fluffy. Beat in eggs. Combine flour and baking powder and add to creamed mixture. Mix sour cream, baking soda and vanilla. Stir into batter and set aside. Combine brown sugar, nuts and cinnamon. Pour half the batter into a greased Bundt pan. Sprinkle with half the nut mixture. Repeat layers. Cut with a thin, sharp knife through the batter to create a marbled effect. Bake at 350 degrees 45 minutes. Dust with powdered sugar.

Yield: 10 to 12 servings

John's Sunday Morning Pancakes

Contributed by John L. Birkinbine, Jr., President of Northfield.

⅔ cup multigrain pancake mix

⅓ cup regular pancake mix

¾ cup 1 percent milk

1 egg

1 tablespoon vegetable oil

¾ cup blueberries, purchased during the summer and frozen in zip-top plastic bags

Spray pan or griddle with non-stick spray. Combine multigrain mix, regular mix, milk, egg and oil. Fold in blueberries. Cook mixture on hot griddle.

Yield: 6-7 large pancakes

Serve with a side of crisp bacon, or scrapple, a Pennsylvania Dutch breakfast meat product produced by Jones Farm and available at Sunset Foods in the frozen meat section.

Rum French Toast

The rum plumps up the raisins for a twist on a
favorite breakfast treat. Cube the bread and soak it overnight in the liquid.
Bake it the next morning for a stuffed style French toast. For a great topping,
heat butter, syrup, sliced bananas and pecan pieces in a pan.
Serve over French toast slices.

6 eggs	1 tablespoon sugar
¼ cup heavy cream	good quality raisin bread or
¼ cup dark rum	day old bread
1 teaspoon ground nutmeg	maple syrup

Whisk together eggs, cream, rum, nutmeg and sugar.
Coat and soak the bread in batter. Cook on a hot griddle. Serve with a
good quality maple syrup.

Yield: 6 to 8 servings

Cape Cod Pancakes

Contributed by Chris and Kate Kennedy.

½ to ¾ cup milk	2 tablespoons sugar
2 tablespoons butter, melted	½ teaspoon salt
1 egg	2 tablespoons sugar
1 cup all-purpose flour	dash of lemon zest
2 teaspoons baking powder	

Combine milk, butter and egg. In separate bowl, combine flour, baking powder, sugar and salt. Stir into creamed mixture. Mix together sugar and zest. Stir into batter. Warm the griddle and pour batter to form individual cakes. Flip when bubbles form all over each pancake. Serve immediately.

Yield: 4 servings

Buttermilk Belgian Waffles

3 cups all-purpose flour,
but may use half white flour
and half whole wheat flour

1 tablespoon baking powder

¾ teaspoon baking soda

1 teaspoon salt

3 tablespoons sugar

3¼ cups buttermilk,
do not use powdered

¾ cup unsalted butter,
melted and cooled

3 large eggs, slightly beaten

2 tablespoons toasted
wheat germ (optional)

Preheat a non-stick Belgian waffle iron. In a large bowl, mix together flour, baking powder, baking soda, sugar and salt. Stir in buttermilk, butter, eggs and wheat germ until smooth. Batter will be thick. Spoon ½ cup batter onto waffle iron and spread out evenly. Transfer to a baking sheet and keep warm in a 200 degree oven.

Yield: 6 to 8 servings

Pure maple syrup is sap that has been boiled until much of the water has evaporated. It has a more subtle flavor and is not as sweet or viscous as artificial maple syrups. The higher the grade of syrup, the lighter the color and more delicate the flavor. Although pure maple syrup is more expensive than its imitators, its flavor is far superior.

Holiday Strata

Serve this with a platter of fresh fruit for a smashing brunch.

4 to 5 cups French bread cubes

1 (8-ounce) package
shredded Cheddar cheese
(2 cups measured)

10 eggs

4 cups milk

1 teaspoon dry mustard

1 teaspoon salt

¼ teaspoon onion powder

8 to 10 slices bacon, cooked
and crumbled

½ cup sliced mushrooms

½ cup chopped tomatoes

Spread bread over the bottom of a greased 13 x 9 x 2-inch baking dish. Top with cheese. Beat together eggs, milk, mustard, salt and onion powder. Pour over cheese. Sprinkle with bacon, mushrooms and tomatoes. Cover and refrigerate up to 24 hours. Uncover and bake at 350 degrees 1 hour. Tent with foil if top browns too quickly.

Yield: 10 to 12 servings

Create a family holiday keepsake with a plain tablecloth or runner in a color appropriate for that holiday by having the kids or all guests sign or write a short note on the runner including the date. Before laundering, embroider the signature, date and/or note written by each guest. Continue the process on each successive holiday. You will have a special reminder of each year and the guests who enjoyed it with you. This is also fun to do with New Years Resolutions if you share that evening with the same people each year.

Hash Brown Quiche

1 (24-ounce) package frozen uncooked shredded hash browns, thawed

5⅓ tablespoons unsalted butter, melted

2 large eggs, beaten

½ cup half-and-half

½ teaspoon seasoned salt

⅛ cup chives, chopped

1 cup shredded jalapeño Jack cheese

1 cup shredded Swiss cheese

1 cup diced ham

fresh parsley for garnish

Press hash browns into quiche pan. Blot with paper towel to remove all moisture. Brush with butter. Bake at 425 degrees 25 minutes. Remove from oven. Reduce oven to 350 degrees. Combine eggs, half-and-half, salt and chives. Sprinkle both cheeses and ham into hash brown shell. Pour egg mixture over top. Bake 40 to 50 minutes. Top with parsley.

Yield: 6 to 8 servings

Grown-Up Grilled Cheese Sandwiches

In the mood for a sandwich but wanting something different?
These grilled cheese sandwiches are just the thing!

- PROVOLONE, BASIL AND ONION ON ITALIAN BREAD -

4 slices thick country Italian bread

1 tablespoon balsamic vinegar

8 thin slices provolone cheese

4 very thin slices red onion, grilled or sautéed for extra flavor

6 to 8 fresh basil leaves

2 slices sweet tomato (optional)

freshly ground pepper

2 tablespoons unsalted butter

Brush each bread slice with a small amount of balsamic vinegar. Arrange two slices of cheese, 2 slices of onion, 3 to 4 fresh basil leaves and a tomato slice on two bread slices. Sprinkle with pepper. Top with remaining bread slices. Melt butter in a cast-iron or non-stick pan over medium high heat. Add sandwiches and cook, pressing down with back of spatula, 2 to 3 minutes per side or until cheese melts and bread is golden brown.

- CHEDDAR, BACON AND APPLE WITH MUSTARD ON WHOLE GRAIN BREAD -

4 thick slices whole grain bread, non-sliced whole grain loaves are available at most grocery stores

2 tablespoons stone-ground or whole grain mustard

6 ounces grated Cheddar, such as aged Vermont

6 slices extra-thick bacon, cooked

1 Granny Smith apple, cut into ¼-inch slices

2 tablespoons butter

Spread each bread slice evenly with mustard. Arrange half the cheese, all the bacon and apple slices on two bread slices. Top with remaining cheese and bread slices and press together gently. Melt butter in large cast-iron or non-stick pan over medium-high heat. Add sandwiches and cook, pressing down with back of spatula, 3 to 5 minutes per side or until cheese melts and bread is buttery and golden brown.

Yield: 2 servings

Smorgastata

This will add an air of sophistication to a brunch or shower.

- EGG LAYER -

10 hard-cooked eggs, chopped
²/₃ cup mayonnaise

2 green onions, chopped
1 teaspoon chopped capers

Combine eggs, mayonnaise, onions and capers.

- SALMON LAYER -

10 ounces smoked salmon
¾ cup crème fraîche

2 teaspoons lemon juice

Mix salmon, crème fraîche and lemon juice.

- CREAM CHEESE LAYER -

¾ cup whipped cream cheese
¼ cup unsalted butter, softened
1 tablespoon chopped dill

1 tablespoon chopped curled parsley
1 tablespoon chopped chives

Blend cream cheese, butter, dill, parsley and chives.

- TOPPING -

⅓ cup chopped dill
⅓ cup chopped curled parsley

⅓ cup chopped chives
2 loaves thin sliced bread

Combine dill, parsley and chives.

- ASSEMBLY - CONSTRUCT ON WAXED OR PARCHMENT PAPER -

Place 8 bread slices lengthwise in a 13 x 9 x 2-inch baking dish. Top with half egg mixture, then bread slices. Top with half salmon mixture, then bread slices. Spread with cream cheese mixture. Top with remaining salmon mixture, and then bread slices. Pour on remaining egg mixture. Sprinkle with topping. Refrigerate at least 12 hours or overnight. Before serving, tidy up with a knife at the sides for clean edges at presentation.

Yield: 16 servings

Potato Quiche Ranchero

This savory quiche is great for brunch or dinner.

½ large white onion, chopped

3 pork sausage patties

6 large eggs

4 cups frozen shredded potatoes or non-seasoned hash browns

1 tablespoon crushed garlic

1 cup shredded Cheddar cheese

½ cup cottage cheese

½ cup chopped green chilies

Salt and pepper to taste

⅛ to ¼ cup chopped cilantro

Cilantro sprigs for garnish

Sauté onions and sausage until done. Drain drippings. Combine onions, sausage, eggs, hash browns, garlic, Cheddar cheese, cottage cheese, chilies, salt, pepper and cilantro. Pour mixture into a greased 11 x 7 x 2-inch baking dish or 10-inch pie plate. Cover and refrigerate overnight. Bake at 350 degrees 50 minutes. Remove foil and bake 10 to 15 minutes more. Serve hot and top with cilantro sprigs.

Yield: 6 servings

Holiday Cheese Puffs

Looking so festive on a plate during the holidays, these go fast!

⅓ cup frozen chopped spinach, thawed and squeezed dry

⅓ cup crumbled blue or feta cheese

¼ cup bacon bits, cooked

1 (2-ounce) jar pimentos, drained

2 tablespoons Ranch dressing

1 sheet frozen puff pastry, thawed

Combine spinach, cheese, bacon, pimentos and dressing until well blended. Cut pastry into twenty-five 2 x 2-inch squares. Spoon 2 teaspoons of mixture onto center of each square. Place squares on a baking sheet. Bake at 400 degrees 20 minutes or until golden browned. Serve warm or room temperature.

Yield: 10 servings

To prevent mold on cheese, wrap it in a cloth dampened with saltwater before refrigerating.

Unbelievable Garlic Spread/Bread

Jazz up any loaf of bread with this spread.

1 French or Italian loaf of bread
½ cup mayonnaise
⅔ cup Parmesan cheese
⅔ cup shredded sharp Cheddar cheese

2 to 4 teaspoons crushed/chopped garlic
dash of Worcestershire sauce
paprika for garnish

Cut loaf in half lengthwise. Blend mayonnaise, Parmesan cheese, Cheddar cheese, garlic and Worcestershire sauce. Spread mixture on each bread half. Broil until bubbly. Serve immediately.

Yield: 10 to 12 servings

Monkey Bread

Sticky, melt in your mouth good!

½ cup chopped pecans
22 frozen yeast rolls
½ (3-ounce) package butterscotch pudding mix, not instant

½ cup butter
¾ cup packed brown sugar
¾ tablespoon cinnamon

Grease a large Bundt pan. Sprinkle nuts on the bottom. Arrange 14 rolls over nuts. Place remaining 8 rolls on top around the center. Sprinkle pudding mix over rolls. Melt butter in a small saucepan. Stir in brown sugar and cinnamon. Pour mixture over rolls. Cover with a towel. Let stand overnight in a cold oven. Uncover. Bake at 350 degrees 30 minutes.

Yield: 8 to 10 servings

Banana and Chocolate Chip Mini-Loaves

A great accompaniment to any brunch or gift basket.
Make these with mini loaf pans for perfect tea slices.

1 teaspoon baking soda	pinch of salt
¼ cup sour cream	1 cup ripe mashed bananas
½ cup butter, softened	1 teaspoon vanilla
1¼ cups sugar	½ cup mini semi-sweet chocolate chip
2 eggs	
1½ cups all-purpose flour	½ cup chopped walnuts or pecans (optional)

In a small bowl, sprinkle baking soda on sour cream and set aside. In a large bowl, cream butter and sugar until fluffy. Add eggs, one at a time, mixing well after each addition. Stir in sour cream mixture. Add flour, salt, bananas and vanilla. Fold in chocolate chips and nuts. Pour batter into greased mini-loaf pans. Bake at 350 degrees 40 to 50 minutes or until toothpick is inserted and comes out clean.

Yield: 3 to 4 loaves

Cranberry Orange Scones

This is a wonderful scone for a holiday brunch.

2 cups all-purpose flour

1 tablespoon baking powder

½ teaspoon baking soda

¼ teaspoon salt

2 tablespoons sugar

1 tablespoon orange zest

½ cup butter, cut into pieces

⅔ cup buttermilk

1 cup dried cranberries

1 tablespoon milk

1 tablespoon sugar

Combine flour, baking powder, baking soda, salt, sugar and zest. Add butter pieces and cut in with a pastry blender until crumbly. Stir in buttermilk and cranberries just until moistened. Turn dough out onto a slightly floured surface. Knead 5 to 6 times. Shape dough into an 8-inch circle. Cut out 8 wedges. Place 1-inch apart on a lightly greased baking sheet. Brush with milk and sprinkle with sugar. Bake at 425 degrees 15 minutes or until golden brown.

Yield: 8 servings

Cream Scones

2 cups all-purpose flour	1/3 cup butter, cut into pieces
1/3 cup sugar	1/2 cup heavy cream
2 teaspoons baking powder	1 large egg
1/8 teaspoon salt	1 teaspoon vanilla

In a large bowl, combine flour, sugar, baking powder and salt.
Add butter with a pastry cutter or two knives until crumbly. In a small
measuring cup, whisk together cream, egg and vanilla until well blended.
Add to flour mixture. Stir until just combined. Knead dough on a lightly
floured surface. Shape dough into a 7-inch circle about 1 1/2 -inches thick.
Cut into 8 wedges. Brush top with remaining egg mixture in bottom of cup.
Place scones on a parchment paper-lined baking sheet. Bake at
375 degrees 15 minutes or until lightly browned.

Yield: 8 servings

Pumpkin Bread

Serve this moist bread as a side with the Harvest Sunset Soup on page 70.

$3\frac{1}{3}$ cups all-purpose flour or wheat flour

1 tablespoon baking soda

1 teaspoon salt

2 cups sugar

1 cup vegetable oil or applesauce

2 cups canned pumpkin

4 eggs

$\frac{2}{3}$ cup water

1 teaspoon ground nutmeg

1 teaspoon cinnamon

$1\frac{1}{4}$ teaspoon ground allspice

Combine flour, baking soda, salt, sugar, oil, pumpkin, eggs and water. Stir in nutmeg, cinnamon and allspice until just well blended. Pour batter into a Bundt pan and one small loaf pan (or three medium loaf pans or four small loaf pans). Bake at 350 degrees at least 1 hour or until toothpick comes out clean. Cool 10 minutes. Remove from pans.

Yield: 15 to 20 servings

Bread may be frozen. Excellent toasted also.

Zucchini Bread

Coconut adds flavor and texture to this bread.

3 eggs	1 teaspoon cinnamon
2 cups sugar	1 teaspoon baking soda
1 cup vegetable oil	1 teaspoon baking powder
2 teaspoons vanilla	1 cup coconut
3 cups all-purpose flour	½ cup nuts, walnuts work well
1 teaspoon salt	3 cups grated zucchini

Beat eggs, sugar, oil and vanilla. Add flour, salt, cinnamon, baking soda, baking powder, coconut, nuts and zucchini. Divide batter into four greased small loaf pans. Bake at 325 degrees 1 hour, 15 minutes.

Yield: 10 to 12 servings

Lemon Raspberry
and Blueberry Jumbo Muffins

Instead of jumbo muffins, you can make 16 regular size muffins.
Baking time is reduced to 18 to 20 minutes.

2 cups all-purpose flour

1 cup sugar

3 teaspoons baking powder

½ teaspoon salt

2 eggs

1 cup half-and-half

½ cup vegetable oil

1 teaspoon lemon extract

½ to 1 teaspoon lemon
zest (optional)

1 cup fresh or frozen unsweetened
raspberries and/or blueberries,
½ cup of each or all of one fruit

white sugar and sliced almonds
for topping

In a large bowl, combine flour, sugar, baking powder and salt. Set aside.
In a small bowl, blend eggs, half-and-half, oil, extract and zest. Stir into dry
ingredients just until moistened. Fold in berries. Spoon batter into greased
jumbo muffin cups, filling two-thirds full. Combine sugar and almonds.
Sprinkle over batter. Bake at 400 degrees 22 to 25 minutes or until toothpick
comes out clean. Cool 5 minutes before removing from pan to
a wire rack. Serve warm.

Yield: 8 jumbo muffins

Appetizers

Baha'i House of Worship and Wilmette Harbor

- Wilmette -

Wilmette

The history of Wilmette is truly a tale of two cities. When Antoine Ouilmette, a French-Canadian fur trader, arrived in Chicago, the Village of Wilmette was born. It is believed that Ouilmette helped the United States to negotiate the 1829 Treaty of Prairie du Chien with the Chippewa, Ottawa, and Potawatomi Indian tribes. In appreciation for his work, he was granted 1,280 acres by the government.

Married to Archange, the daughter of a Frenchman and Potawatomi Indian, Ouilmette sold his land when the Potawatomi Indian tribe began their western migration. At about the same time, a group of immigrants from Trier, Germany settled into a farming community just west of the Ouilmette reservation. The immigrants will always be remembered by the nationally revered New Trier High School, which currently educates students from five North Shore Villages.

Incorporated in 1872, the village was named Wilmette, a tribute to its earlier settlers. Attracting many new families to the area, the railroad helped Wilmette develop into a burgeoning suburb.

Wilmette continues to celebrate and embrace its diverse cultural environment. The first of its kind in the Western Hemisphere, the Baha'i House of Worship has become a prominent landmark in Wilmette. Although the lakeside Village of Wilmette has grown considerably from its early days, it has retained the dynamic spirit of the men and women who shaped the North Shore.

 Halloween Supper

On this brisk, late afternoon, costumed children race
from house to house while their parents watch from the sidewalk.
Come home to a feast that children of all ages will enjoy.

Sunshine Punch

Goat Cheese Terrine

Harvest Sunset Soup

Herb Roasted Pork with New Potatoes

Candy Shop Pizza

Grilled Soft-Shelled Crabs

Contributed by Christopher S. Canning, President of Wilmette.

This is a great summertime appetizer. It is a great way to bring the taste of the ocean to the North Shore.

juice of 4 limes	¼ cup coriander
½ cup golden tequila	½ cup olive oil
1 garlic clove, minced	salt and pepper to taste
1 jalapeño pepper, seeded and minced or 1 tablespoon chili powder	8 soft-shell crabs, dressed

Whisk together lime juice, tequila, garlic, pepper and coriander. Gradually whisk in olive oil. Season with salt and pepper. Place crabs in a single layer in a shallow bowl. Pour marinade over crabs. Cover and refrigerate at least 20 minutes. Remove crabs from marinade, reserving marinade. Place crabs 3 to 4 inches from heat. Grill 2 to 3 minutes per side until cooked through. Transfer to a serving platter. Pour marinade into a serving bowl and place in center of platter for dipping. Serve immediately.

Yield: 8 servings

Santa Fe Shrimp Cocktail

Contributed by Chef Jeffrey Tomchek of Deer Path Inn, Lake Forest.

Summer is the season for fresh rock shrimp from Florida.
This dish makes a great first course for a summer barbecue. You can
also serve a larger portion as an entrée for lunch.

½ pound rock shrimp, peeled and deveined

1 tablespoon olive oil

2 cups clamato juice

1 tablespoon Worcestershire sauce

1 ripe avocado, peeled, seeded and diced

¼ bunch fresh cilantro, minced

¼ cup red onion, minced

1 Anaheim Chile, roasted, peeled, seeded and minced

juice of 1 lime

salt and white pepper to taste

ground cumin to taste

lime wedges and cilantro sprigs

blue corn tortilla chips or saltines

Cook the shrimp following the technique in the Chef's Tip.
Combine shrimp, olive oil, lime juice, Worcestershire sauce, avocado,
cilantro, onions, chile, juice, salt, pepper and cumin. Garnish with lime
wedges and cilantro. Serve with blue corn tortilla chips or saltines.

Yield: 4 servings

*Chef's Tip: For perfectly cooked shrimp bring the cooking liquid to a boil.
Prepare an ice bath of equal parts water and ice, large enough to hold all the
shrimp. Add the shrimp to the boiling water. As soon as the water comes back
to a boil remove the shrimp and place immediately in the ice bath. Drain the
cooked shrimp and proceed with your recipe.*

*Chef Jeffrey Tomchek likes to serve this with Margaritas,
ice cold Mexican beer or Sangria.*

Tailgate Appetizer: Sausage Bread

Contributed by Aaron and Emery Moorehead.

Who would know more about game-day food than
Chicago Bear's Super Bowl XX champion Emery Moorehead and his son,
Aaron, wide receiver for the Indianapolis Colts?

2 pounds pork sausage

3 eggs, beaten, reserve ⅛ cup

1 (8-ounce) package
shredded Cheddar cheese

1 (8-ounce) package shredded
mozzarella cheese

2 tablespoons Parmesan cheese

1 teaspoon garlic salt

1 teaspoon dried oregano

1 teaspoon dried parsley

1 teaspoon salt

4 (8-ounce) packages
refrigerated crescent rolls

Brown and drain sausage. Add eggs, Cheddar cheese,
mozzarella cheese, Parmesan cheese, garlic salt, oregano, parsley and salt.
Mix well. Unroll each dough roll on parchment paper and flatten into four
rectangles. Divide sausage mixture between rectangles. Roll up long sides
of dough sealing edges. Place seam side down on a baking sheet.
Brush tops with reserved egg. Bake at 375 degrees 20 minutes or until
golden browned. Slice and serve.

Yield: 4 loaves

Crostini Di Polenta Con Caprini

(Polenta Crostini with Goat Cheese)

Contributed by North Shore Community Bank's Customer Celebrity Chef,
Nancy Brussat Barocci of Convito Italiano and Betise in Wilmette.

- POLENTA -

2 quarts milk	$\frac{1}{2}$ teaspoon nutmeg
4 ounces butter	$\frac{3}{4}$ pound yellow cornmeal
1 tablespoon salt	

Heat milk and butter in a saucepan. When it comes to a boil, add the
salt and nutmeg and begin to gradually incorporate the corn meal, using a
whip. When mixture begins to thicken, decrease heat and simmer, stirring
constantly with a wooden spoon for 15 to 20 minutes. Lightly butter an
18 x 12- inch cookie sheet with sides and pour the polenta mixture
into a pan, spreading evenly with a spatula.

- TOPPING -

3 pounds ripe plum tomatoes, thinly sliced	54 small fresh basil leaves or 54 pieces
1½ pounds Caprini (Italian Goat cheese) or domestic goat cheese	extra virgin olive oil

Spread goat cheese over polenta. Then layer the plum tomatoes on top of
the goat cheese, slightly overlapping them. Bake in a 350 degree oven for
25 minutes. When cooled cut into 2-inch squares. Remove from the pan
and garnish each with a basil leaf that has been dipped into olive oil.

Yield: 54 (2-inch) squares

Sea Scallop Appetizer with
Goat Cheese and Garlic-Butter Sauce

Submitted by The Noodle in Wilmette.

½ tablespoon minced garlic

½ cup butter, softened

1 cup margarine

2 tablespoons Parmesan cheese

3 tablespoons chopped fresh parsley, divided

Juice of 1 lemon

¼ teaspoon salt

¼ teaspoon cracked black pepper

¼ cup all-purpose flour, seasoned with salt and pepper

12 large sea scallops

¼ cup olive oil

½ cup goat cheese

½ cup plain dry bread crumbs

½ cup melted butter

Lemon wedges, for garnish

Parsley springs, for garnish

Combine garlic, softened butter, margarine, Parmesan, 1 tablespoon chopped parsley, lemon juice, salt and pepper in a medium mixing bowl. With electric mixer on high speed, whip mixture for five minutes. When softened and well-blended, set aside. Preheat oven to broil. Place seasoned flour on a plate and dredge scallops. In large, shallow skillet, bring olive oil to high heat. Place scallops in skillet and sauté for 40 seconds on each side. Remove scallops from pan and transfer to a baking sheet. Sprinkle browned scallops with goat cheese and bread crumbs; place ½ to ¾ tablespoon of reserved butter mixture on each one. Sprinkle remaining parsley over pan and broil for 3½ to 4 minutes. To serve, arrange 3 scallops in center of plate; drizzle with melted butter and garnish with lemon wedges and a sprig of parsley.

Yield: 4 servings

Canadian Pâté

Serve with a variety of good mustards.

4 to 5 slices double smoked bacon
or 2 slices pork sausage, not spicy

8 ounces organic chicken livers

6 to 8 tablespoons butter

¼ cup brandy

1 large onion, chopped

3 stalks celery, chopped

1 bay leaf

salt and pepper to taste

large handful parsley, chopped

Cook bacon until done. Remove from pan and pour out grease. Brown livers with 2 to 4 tablespoons butter until cooked through. Return bacon and add brandy. Cook until liquid is absorbed. Remove meat and sauté onions and celery in remaining butter. Return meat to pan. Add bay leaf, salt and pepper. Simmer 20 minutes. Stir in parsley and simmer an additional 5 minutes. Remove bay leaf. Pour mixture into blender. Blend until smooth. Refrigerate at least 3 hours.

Yield: 10 to 12 servings

Fiesta Shrimp

A huge hit!

1 pound large shrimp, cooked
without tails

½ teaspoon lime zest

¼ cup lime juice

2 tablespoons olive oil

2 tablespoons finely chopped
green onions

¼ cup chopped Anaheim or
jalapeño pepper

1 to 2 tablespoons snipped cilantro

2 garlic cloves, minced or
2 teaspoons prepared garlic

½ teaspoon sugar

½ teaspoon salt

¼ teaspoon pepper

lettuce leaves

papaya slices for garnish

Combine shrimp, zest, juice, olive oil, onions, peppers, cilantro, garlic, sugar, salt and pepper in a zip-top plastic bag. Marinate in the refrigerator, turning every few hours. Serve on lettuce leaves and garnish with papaya.

Yield: 6 to 8 servings

Spicy Nuts

Serve these nuts slightly warm with cocktails. We find them addicting and so will your guests. Wrap them up and they serve as a delightful host or hostess gift.

1 (18-ounce) container mixed nuts

2 tablespoons chopped fresh rosemary

1 teaspoon cayenne pepper

2 teaspoons brown sugar

2 teaspoons sea salt

1 teaspoon butter, melted

Spread nuts in a single layer on a baking sheet. Toast at 350 degrees 10 minutes. Combine rosemary, cayenne, brown sugar, salt and butter in a large bowl. Add nuts and toss to coat. Serve warm.

Yield: 6 servings

Red Pepper Bruschetta

A crowd pleasing first course.

1 (6-ounce) package shredded Parmesan, Romano or feta cheese

1 cup chopped roasted peppers, drained

½ cup chopped green onions

1 tablespoon olive oil, plus additional set aside

2 garlic cloves, minced

2 teaspoons balsamic vinegar

1 loaf French bread, cut into ½-inch slices

Combine cheese, peppers, onions, oil, garlic and vinegar. Brush bread with oil that was set aside. Spoon 1 tablespoon of mixture on each bread slice. Toast under broiler until lightly browned.

Yield: 8 to 10 servings

Black Bean and Corn Salsa

This is a great salsa and even better
when served with the Lemonade Mojitos on page 233.

1 (15-ounce) can black beans, drained and rinsed

1 (15-ounce) can white corn, drained

3 Roma tomatoes, chopped

⅔ cup chopped green onions

⅔ cup chopped cilantro

¼ cup olive oil

¼ cup red wine vinegar

2 garlic cloves, minced

1 teaspoon ground cumin

1 medium avocado, chopped

tortilla chips

Combine beans, corn, tomatoes, onions and cilantro. Whisk together oil, vinegar, garlic and cumin to create dressing. Add dressing to bean mixture. Stir in avocado before serving. May be made in advance. Serve with tortilla chips or as a side garnish.

Yield: 6 to 8 servings

Ginger Cheese

An exotic first course.

1 (8-ounce) package cream cheese, softened

2 tablespoons half-and-half

3 tablespoons chopped crystallized ginger

2 tablespoons sliced almonds, toasted

gingersnaps

Blend cream cheese and half-and-half with electric mixer at medium speed until smooth. Stir in ginger. Refrigerate 8 hours. Sprinkle with almonds. Serve with gingersnaps.

Yield: 6 to 8 servings

Pineapple Cheese Ball

A great addition to any brunch.

1 (8-ounce) package cream
cheese, softened
4 green onions, chopped

1 (20-ounce) can crushed
pineapple, drained
chopped walnuts
assorted crackers

Combine cream cheese, onions and three-fourths of the can of pineapple.
Shape mixture into a ball. Roll ball in walnuts. Refrigerate 3 to 4 hours.
Serve with crackers.

Yield: 6 to 8 servings

Curry Pâté

Simple and full of flavor!

1 (8-ounce) package cream
cheese, softened
$\frac{1}{3}$ cup mild chutney
1 teaspoon dry mustard

2 teaspoons mild curry powder
$\frac{1}{4}$ cup chopped pecans
assorted crackers

Blend together cream cheese, chutney, mustard and curry.
Shape into a mold and refrigerate at least 4 hours. Sprinkle pecans on top.
Serve with crackers.

Yield: 4 to 6 servings

Cheese and Berry Canapés

This one was the highlight of conversation at many of our League meetings.
The cheese and strawberry go hand in hand in this dish.

2 (8-ounce) packages shredded
sharp Cheddar cheese
1 cup pecans, chopped
¾ cup mayonnaise
1 medium onion, grated

1 garlic clove, pressed
1 teaspoon Tabasco sauce
1 cup strawberry preserves
individual mini pastry cups

Combine cheese, pecans, mayonnaise, onions, garlic, Tabasco and
preserves and mix well. Spoon mixture into pastry cups just before serving.
Can make cheese and berry mixture the day before serving.

Yield: 8 to 10 servings

Goat Cheese Terrine

4 ounces chèvre goat
cheese, softened
4 ounces cream cheese, softened
½ cup stick butter, softened

pesto
sun-dried tomatoes,
drained and chopped
pine nuts (optional)

Beat together goat cheese, cream cheese and butter. Line mold with
cheesecloth. Spread one-third cheese mixture on bottom of mold. Top with
pesto and another layer of cheese. Spread with sun-dried tomatoes and top
with a layer of cheese mixture. Cover with cheesecloth and refrigerate
2 hours. To serve, invert mold onto plate and remove cheesecloth.
Top with pine nuts.

Yield: 4 to 6 servings

Cinco de Mayo Dip

This one is great served with margaritas.

1 (8-ounce) package
cream cheese, softened

½ cup sour cream

1 (6-ounce) can avocado dip

½ (1-ounce) package
taco seasoning mix

2 (8-ounce) packages
shredded Cheddar cheese

2 large tomatoes, chopped

1 bunch green onions, chopped

1 (4-ounce) can chopped olives

corn chips

Blend cream cheese, sour cream, avocado dip and seasoning until smooth. Refrigerate several hours or overnight. Spread on serving dish. Top with a layer of each of cheese, tomatoes, onions and olives. Serve with corn chips.

Yield: 6 to 8 servings

Shrimp Dip

*A southern classic. Recipe may be made two days
in advance and doubled. May also use fresh cooked shrimp.*

1 (8-ounce) package
cream cheese, softened

⅓ cup mayonnaise

3 tablespoons chili sauce

2 teaspoons lemon juice

1 teaspoon minced onions

1 teaspoon Worcestershire sauce

½ teaspoon curry powder

1 (4½-ounce) can shrimp

corn chips or crackers

Blend cream cheese, mayonnaise, chili sauce, juice, onions, Worcestershire sauce, curry and shrimp with an electric mixer. Refrigerate at least 3 hours. Serve with corn chips or crackers.

Yield: 6 to 8 servings

Gourmet Guacamole

Not your usual guacamole.

3 large tomatoes, chopped

3 large avocados, chopped

4 green onions, chopped

1 (4-ounce) can olives, chopped and drained

3 tablespoons vegetable oil

1½ tablespoons apple cider vinegar

1 teaspoon salt

1 teaspoon garlic salt

¼ teaspoon pepper

tortilla chips

Combine tomatoes, avocados, onions and olives. Blend oil, vinegar, salt, garlic salt and pepper. Drizzle over tomato mixture and toss gently. Cover and refrigerate no longer than 4 hours. Serve with tortilla chips.

Yield: 6 servings

Made a perfect batch of guacamole and don't want it to turn brown? Save the pit and place in the middle of the dip. This will increase its lifespan.

Herbed Mushrooms

1 (16-ounce) package mushrooms, rinsed

1 (5-ounce) package herbed goat cheese (Boursin), softened

2 tablespoons olive oil

Remove stems and inside of mushrooms. Spoon cheese into mushrooms until slightly bulging out of top. Place on a baking sheet and drizzle with oil. Bake at 350 degrees 20 minutes until mushrooms have cooked and cheese mixture is slightly toasted.

Yield: 6 servings

Caramelized Onion
and Goat Cheese Tarts

Caramelized onions add boldness and richness to recipes.
They accompany the goat cheese perfectly in these beautiful tarts.

1 tablespoon unsalted butter
1 large onion, thinly sliced
¼ cup white wine
½ teaspoon chopped fresh
thyme leaves

¼ cup soft mild goat
cheese, softened
mini pastry shells
chopped thyme leaves for garnish

Heat butter in a heavy skillet over moderately high heat until foam subsides. Sauté onions, stirring occasionally, until golden brown. Add wine and deglaze skillet, scraping up any brown bits and cooking until liquid evaporates. Stir in thyme and cook until onion is deep golden brown. Place a dollop of goat cheese and spoonful of onion mixture in pastry shells. Place on a buttered baking sheet. Bake at 350 degrees 10 minutes or until warm. Garnish tarts with thyme and serve immediately.

Yield: 8 to 10 servings

Sausage Bites in Bourbon Sauce on a Bed of Sweet Potatoes

All the best flavors of the Deep South in one bite.

1 cup packed brown sugar

1 cup bourbon

1 cup chili sauce

3 pounds smoked sausage links, cut into bite size pieces

3 pounds sliced sweet potatoes, sliced ¼ -inch thick

olive oil

salt and herbs de Provence to taste

Combine brown sugar, bourbon and chili sauce. Pour over sausage. Cover and refrigerate overnight. Arrange potato slices in a baking dish. Drizzle with oil. Sprinkle with salt and herbs. Roast at 350 degrees 25 minutes or until crispy. Cool. Bake sausage at 325 degrees 2 hours, 30 minutes. Pierce 1 to 2 sausage pieces on a toothpick and top with a sweet potato round. Serve warm.

Yield: 10 to 12 servings

In 1893, a unique popcorn, peanuts and molasses confection was introduced by F.W. Rueckheim and Brother at the World's Columbian Exposition, Chicago's first World's Fair. It was such a hit that someone said, "That's Cracker Jack."

Twice Baked Potato Appetizer

Another crowd pleaser. A bite size version of everyone's favorite potato.

1½ pounds small red potatoes

2 tablespoons vegetable oil

1 cup shredded Monterey Jack cheese

½ cup sour cream

1 (3-ounce) package cream cheese, softened

⅓ cup minced green onions

1 teaspoon dried basil

1 garlic clove, minced

½ teaspoon salt

¼ teaspoon pepper

Pierce potatoes and rub skins with oil. Place in a 13 x 9 x 2-inch baking dish. Bake at 400 degrees 50 minutes or until tender. Cool. Combine Jack cheese, sour cream, cream cheese, onions, basil, garlic, salt and pepper. Cut potatoes in half. Carefully scoop out pulp and add to cheese mixture. Mash together until smooth. Spoon mixture into potato skins. Broil 7 to 8 minutes or until heated through.

Yield: 12 servings

Spinach and Artichoke Dip

Not your typical artichoke dip.

2 (10-ounce) packages frozen chopped spinach, thawed and squeezed dry

1 tablespoon minced garlic

2 tablespoons minced onion

¼ cup butter

¼ cup all-purpose flour

1 pint heavy cream

¼ cup chicken stock

2 teaspoons lemon juice

½ teaspoon Tabasco sauce

½ teaspoon salt

⅔ cup grated Pecorino Romano cheese

¼ cup sour cream

1 (12-ounce) jar artichoke hearts, drained and coarsely chopped

1 cup shredded sharp white Cheddar cheese

tortilla chips

Mince spinach. Sauté garlic and onions in butter 3 to 5 minutes until golden brown. Stir in flour and cook 1 minute. Slowly whisk in cream and stock. Bring to boil. Stir in lemon juice, Tabasco, salt and Romano cheese. Stir until cheese melts. Remove from heat and cool 5 minutes. Stir in sour cream. Fold in spinach and artichokes. Pour mixture into a microwave safe pie plate. Sprinkle with Cheddar cheese. Microwave to melt cheese. Serve with tortilla chips.

Yield: 8 to 12 servings

Buffalo Chicken Dip

This makes for great tailgate fare.

1 pound boneless, skinless chicken breast halves

1 (8-ounce) package cream cheese, softened

1 cup blue cheese dressing

½ (12-ounce) jar Buffalo style red hot sauce

1 cup shredded Cheddar cheese

tortilla chips or corn chip scoops

Boil chicken until cooked through. Shred chicken. Combine chicken, cream cheese, blue cheese dressing and hot sauce. Spoon mixture into a 13 x 9 x 2-inch baking dish. Sprinkle with cheese. Bake at 350 degrees 25 minutes or until cheese melts and is bubbly. Serve with tortilla chips or corn chips.

Yield: 6 to 8 servings

Warm Crab and Artichoke Dip

A rich and tasty hot dip for a cool winter day.

½ (8-ounce) package cream cheese, softened

½ cup mayonnaise

salt and pepper to taste

¾ cup crabmeat, drained

¼ cup Parmesan cheese

3 tablespoons chopped marinated artichoke hearts, drained

2 tablespoons sliced green onions

2 tablespoons diced red bell pepper

2 tablespoons diced celery

1 tablespoon finely chopped Italian parsley

1½ teaspoons sherry or red wine vinegar

¼ teaspoon Tabasco sauce

2 tablespoons Parmesan cheese

toasted baguette slices or bagel chips

Beat cream cheese until smooth. Blend in mayonnaise. Add salt and pepper. Fold in crabmeat, ¼ cup Parmesan cheese, artichokes, onions, peppers, celery, parsley, sherry and Tabasco. Spoon mixture into a 2 cup soufflé dish. Top with Parmesan cheese. Bake at 400 degrees 15 minutes until cheese melts. Transfer to a platter. Serve immediately with baguette slices.

Yield: 4 to 6 servings

Soups

The Glenview Historical Society

- Glenview -

Glenview

The first European settlers arrived in the area now known as Glenview soon after the Native Americans were relocated following the Treaty of Chicago in 1833. Most of the early settlers arrived from England and Germany, purchasing farmland at $1.25 per acre. Agriculture continued to be the primary industry well into the twentieth century.

In the early years, Glenview had many names; South Northfield, Oak Glen and Barr. At the time of incorporation in 1899, the name Glenview was officially chosen. Much of the area's early prosperity and expansion developed as a result of the construction of the Chicago, Milwaukee, St. Paul and Pacific Railroads.

One of the earliest settlers to the area, the Kennicott family, built their home, The Grove, which is now a National Landmark. A son, Robert Kennicott, became a world renowned naturalist. Another prominent family in the area, the Hutchings, owned the farmland that is now downtown Glenview. Their homestead is now the home to the Glenview Historical Society.

In 1929, the Curtiss Reynolds Air Force was built and later became home to the Naval Air Station Glenview. The Base, as it is known locally, played a vital role during World War II. Most carrier pilots received their qualification training in Glenview. Some notable pilots that came through The Base are Gerald Ford, George Bush, and Neil Armstrong.

Following closure of the Base in 1993, the area has been redeveloped with beautiful new homes, golf courses, elegant shops and restaurants, resulting in a dramatic population increase in the village.

Cinco De Mayo

The perfect balance of lively and tasty. Olé!

Gourmet Guacamole

Cinco de Mayo Dip

Fiesta Shrimp

Chicken Enchiladas

Roasted Corn Salad

Tropical Fruit Salad

Ancho Chile Devil's Food Cake

Caramel Pecan Triangles

Upstate New York Minestrone Soup

Contributed by the Glenview Historical Society.

Delicious! May be frozen.

1 pound Italian sweet sausage

1 tablespoon olive oil or vegetable oil

1 cup diced onion

1 garlic clove, minced

1 cup sliced carrots

1 teaspoon dried crumbled basil

2 small zucchini, sliced

1 (16-ounce) can Italian pear or Roma tomatoes, chopped, undrained

2 (10¾-ounce) cans beef stock or 3 beef bouillon cubes and 1½ cups of hot water

2 cups shredded cabbage

1 teaspoon salt

¼ teaspoon pepper

½ teaspoon Tabasco sauce

1 tablespoon Worcestershire sauce

1 (15-ounce) can great Northern beans, undrained

chopped fresh parsley, about a handful

French bread slices or hard rolls

Slice sausage crosswise, about ½-inch thick. Brown in oil in large stockpot or Dutch oven. (May also cover sausage with small amount of water and cook until water evaporates, allowing sausage to brown.) Add onions, garlic, carrots and basil. Cook 5 minutes. Stir in zucchini, tomatoes, stock, cabbage, salt, pepper, Tabasco and Worcestershire sauce. Bring to boil. Reduce heat, cover and simmer 1 hour. Add beans and parsley. Cook at reduced heat another 20 minutes. Serve with French bread or hard rolls.

Yield: 8 servings

Tortilla Soup

Contributed by David Jones, CFO and Director of Operations of Food2You Catering in Chicago. David is also well known for developing and launching chef-driven restaurants in the Chicago and North Shore area.

2 tablespoons olive oil

2 tablespoons butter

2 large red or yellow onions, coarsely chopped

4 whole jalapeño peppers, halved

1 (28-ounce) can whole peeled tomatoes with juice

6 (14-ounce) cans chicken stock

2 bunches fresh cilantro

8 corn tortillas or 40 tortilla chips

salt and pepper to taste

Heat a large stockpot on medium-high heat. Add oil and butter. Sauté onions, salt and pepper until tender but not browned. Most of the heat in a jalapeño is in the seed and white ribs inside. Depending on your taste, remove seeds and ribs from 1 to 3 of the four peppers. Wash your hands carefully afterward. You may want to use gloves if your skin is sensitive. Add to onions and cook until soft. Be careful not to touch your eyes when cleaning hot peppers. Rinse cilantro, set aside some nicer pieces for garnish. Trim heavy stems from the cilantro and discard. Add remaining cleaned cilantro leaves and fine stems to pot. There should still be moisture in the pot from all of the vegetable sweating. Add tortillas or tortilla chips, stir into mixture until they start to break down. Stir in tomatoes and mix well. Add stock and mix well. Bring to boil. Remove from heat. Purée with immersion blender for several minutes until soup reaches desired consistency. Remember that the soup is boiling hot, so be very careful.

Yield: 6 to 8 servings

Pumpkin Chowder

Contributed by Chef Jeffrey Tomchek of Deer Path Inn, Lake Forest.

This will also work well with Hubbard Pumpkin, Queensland Squash or Sweet Mama Squash.

Beverage Recommendation: Try a white Bordeaux or Alsatian Gewürztraminer from France.

1 small pie pumpkin

sea salt and pepper to taste

4 ears sweet corn, husked and silk removed

3 quarts whipping cream

8 to 10 slices bacon Applewood smoked bacon, minced

2 sticks unsalted butter

1 red bell pepper, minced

½ cup minced yellow onion

½ cup minced celery

½ cup minced carrots

2 tablespoons minced rosemary

chopped chives or Italian parsley

Split pumpkin and remove seeds. Season pumpkin with salt and pepper. Roast at 500 degrees until nicely caramelized. Remove pumpkin pulp and reserve. Cut kernels from cob and reserve. Cut up cobs and simmer with cream 2 hours. In a heavy stockpot, cook bacon in butter until crisp. Remove bacon and reserve. Add peppers, onions, celery, carrots, corn and rosemary to pan. Sauté until lightly caramelized. Set aside. Strain cobs from cream and add cream to the pumpkin pulp. Purée mixture until smooth. Transfer to vegetable mixture. Simmer 30 minutes. Add salt and pepper. To serve, sprinkle reserved bacon and chives or Italian parsley over each portion. Serve immediately.

Yield: 8 servings

Curried Mushroom Soup

Contributed by Three Tarts Bakery and Café, Northfield.

3 tablespoons unsalted butter

1 large Spanish onion, diced

1 stalk celery, diced

2 garlic cloves, minced

pinch of kosher salt

1 pound mushrooms, sliced

1½ teaspoons curry powder

2 tablespoons all-purpose flour

4 cups chicken stock

2 cups of hot water

¼ pound mushrooms, sliced

1 cup heavy cream

kosher salt and white pepper to taste

In a large stockpot, melt butter over medium heat. Sauté onions, celery, garlic and salt for 15 minutes, stirring occasionally. Add mushrooms and salt. Cook 10 minutes more, stirring occasionally. Stir in curry and cook 1 minute. Stir in flour and cook 2 minutes. Slowly stir in stock and cook 20 minutes stirring occasionally. Using an immersion blender, purée soup until smooth. Stir in up to 2 cups of hot water to thin the mushroom purée. Set aside over low heat. In a small non-stick skillet over medium heat, dry sauté mushrooms for 10 minutes until soft. Add to stockpot. Stir in cream. Add salt and white pepper. Heat thoroughly before serving. Serve at room temperature.

Yield: 6 to 8 servings

White Bean Chicken Chili

Hearty and healthy.

1 (1-pound) package boneless, skinless chicken breast halves

2 to 4 (15-ounce) cans great Northern beans, undrained

1 (24-ounce) jar medium salsa

2 to 5 teaspoons ground cumin

1 (8-ounce) block jalapeño Monterey Jack cheese, cubed

sour cream, corn bread or tortilla chips for garnish

Cover chicken with water. Boil until cooked through. Remove chicken to cool. Reserve cooking water. Shred chicken with a fork. In a large stockpot, combine chicken, beans, salsa, cumin and enough cooking water to reach desired thickness. Simmer until thoroughly heated. Just prior to serving, add cheese cubes. Stir until melted. Serve with sour cream, corn bread or tortilla chips.

Yield: 4 to 6 servings

Split Pea Soup

Nothing will warm you up more than a bowl of this wonderful soup.

1 pound split peas (picked and rinsed)

8 cups water

1 ham hock or meaty ham bone

1 to 2 bay leaves

5 whole peppercorns

1 cup chopped onions

1 cup chopped celery

1 cup chopped carrots

1 teaspoon garlic pepper salt

Combine peas, water, ham, bay leaves, peppercorns, onions, celery, carrots and garlic salt. Bring to boil. Reduce heat and simmer, stirring frequently, at least 1 hour or until smooth and peas are tender. Remove ham bone and bay leaves. Add ham meat before serving. Soup will be very thick.

Yield: 4 servings

Curried Lentil Soup

Well worth the effort and it freezes well.

- LENTILS -

½ teaspoon olive oil

1 medium onion, diced

1 garlic clove, minced

1 tablespoon chopped thyme

½ cup lentils, rinsed

1 teaspoon curry powder

pinch of pepper

1 tablespoon soy sauce

3 cups vegetable stock

Heat oil in a large stockpot. Sauté onions, garlic and thyme 5 minutes or until golden brown. Add lentils, curry, pepper, soy sauce and stock. Bring to boil. Reduce heat and simmer 45 minutes or until lentils are al dente. Lentils should be covered with stock while cooking. Set aside.

- VEGETABLES -

½ teaspoon olive oil

1 medium onion, diced

1 stalk celery, diced

1 red or yellow bell pepper, diced

1 medium tomato, diced

½ cup thinly sliced
   shiitake mushrooms

3 garlic cloves, minced

1 tablespoon chopped oregano

1 teaspoon soy sauce

Heat oil in a large skillet. Sauté onions, celery and peppers 5 minutes or until golden brown. Add tomatoes, mushrooms, garlic, oregano and soy sauce. Cook 2 to 3 minutes more. Stir vegetables into lentils. Simmer 5 minutes.

Yield: 6 to 8 servings

Spicy Thai Chowder

It is savory, it is creamy and it is excellent!

1 medium onion, diced
½ large red bell pepper, diced
⅛ teaspoon ground turmeric
1 tablespoon butter
1 (14-ounce) can baby corn
1 pound new potatoes,
  peeled and diced small
3 cups chicken stock

1 cup unsweetened coconut milk
1 tablespoon chili garlic sauce
1½ tablespoons Asian fish sauce
½ tablespoon brown sugar
1 tablespoon lemon juice
1 pound sea scallops
1 cup chopped bok choy

Sauté onions, peppers and turmeric in butter 5 to 8 minutes.
Add corn, potatoes and stock. Bring to boil. Cook 5 to 8 minutes until
potatoes are tender. Use back of spoon to mash some potatoes to thicken
soup. Stir in coconut milk and return to boil. Immediately reduce heat and
add chili sauce, fish sauce, brown sugar and juice. Stir until well blended.
Add scallops and bok choy. Return to boil for 1 minute.
Remove from heat. Serve hot.

Yield: 4 to 6 servings

Tomato-Basil Soup

A classic. Try this with our Grown Up Grilled
Cheese Sandwiches on page 25.

1 small onion, chopped

2 to 3 garlic cloves, chopped

1 tablespoon olive oil

1 pound tomatoes, chopped

½ cup tomato sauce

¾ cup chicken stock

¼ cup heavy cream

2 tablespoons coarsely
chopped fresh basil

2 tablespoons Parmesan cheese

salt and pepper to taste

pesto (optional)

1 thick-sliced toasted Italian
bread, cubed

Sauté onions and garlic in oil until tender. Add tomatoes and
cook 10 minutes. Stir in tomato sauce, stock, cream and half the basil.
Simmer 30 minutes and remove from heat. Transfer to blender. Purée
until smooth. Return to pan. Add remaining basil, Parmesan cheese, salt
and pepper. Garnish individual servings with a dollop of
pesto and top with bread cubes.

Yield: 4 servings

Harvest Sunset Soup

Serve with toasted pumpkin bread.

¼ cup diced celery

½ cup diced onions

¼ cup diced carrots

¼ cup diced leeks (bulb)

2 tablespoons unsalted butter

½ cup all-purpose flour

2 quarts chicken stock

ground mace, cinnamon and nutmeg to taste

kosher salt and freshly ground pepper to taste

2 cups fresh pumpkin or butternut squash, peeled and diced

¼ pound Brie cheese, rind removed and diced

¼ pound Gruyère cheese, grated

¼ cup Frangelico liqueur

1 cup heavy cream

1 tablespoon unsalted butter

Combine celery, onions, carrots, leeks and butter in a stockpot. Sauté until soft but not brown. Whisk in flour and cook 2 minutes. Gradually stir in stock and add mace, cinnamon, nutmeg, salt and pepper. Bring to boil and add pumpkin. Reduce heat and simmer 40 minutes or until pumpkin is soft. Add Brie, Gruyère and Frangelico. Simmer 5 to 7 minutes or until both cheeses melt. Stir in cream and additional butter, if desired.

Yield: 8 to 10 servings

Zucchini Soup

This is heaven in a bowl.

2 pounds Italian sausage, regular or turkey

2 cups chopped celery

2 pounds zucchini, chopped

2 (28-ounce) cans Italian diced tomatoes

1 teaspoon Italian seasoning

1 teaspoon sugar

¼ teaspoon garlic powder

1 cup chopped onions

2 teaspoons salt

1 teaspoon dried oregano

½ teaspoon dried basil

2 bell peppers, diced

Parmesan cheese for garnish

Remove casing from sausage. Roll into small balls. Brown sausage in a large stockpot or Dutch oven. Drain off excess fat. Add celery and simmer 10 minutes, stirring occasionally. Stir in zucchini, tomatoes, seasoning, sugar, garlic powder, onions, salt, oregano and basil. Simmer 20 minutes. Add peppers. Cover and cook 10 minutes more. Top with Parmesan cheese.

Yield: 6 to 8 servings

Turkey Corn Chowder

Turkey makes this a hearty meal.

3 slices bacon, cut into ¼ -inch pieces
2 cups chopped onions
¾ cup thinly sliced celery
1 garlic clove, minced
2 cups turkey or chicken stock (see note below)

3 cups skinned and diced potatoes
pinch of crushed red pepper
1 cup whole kernel corn
½ cup milk
1½ cups cooked and cubed turkey
salt and pepper to taste
chopped parsley for garnish

Cook bacon in a large stockpot until crisp. Add onions, celery and garlic. Cook 10 to 12 minutes on low heat. Stir in stock, potatoes and red pepper. Bring to boil. Reduce heat, cover and simmer 15 minutes or until potatoes are tender. Add corn, milk and turkey. Stir in salt and pepper and cook 2 to 3 minutes until warm. Garnish with parsley just before serving.

Yield: 4 servings

Make stock by simmering turkey bones
with half an onion, peppercorns and celery in water.

Lamb Stew

3 pounds lamb-stew meat, cut into 2-inch chunks

2 tablespoons all-purpose flour

1 tablespoon dried oregano

1 tablespoon kosher salt

½ teaspoon freshly ground black pepper

3 to 6 tablespoons olive oil

4 carrots, peeled and cut into ½-inch thick slices

4 stalks celery, diced

1 to 2 cups of cubed potatoes

3 medium onions, sliced

4 garlic cloves, crushed

1 (750-milliliter) bottle full-bodied red wine, such as Côtes du Rhône or Cabernet Sauvignon

2 bay leaves

4 strips fresh lemon peel

Pat the lamb with paper towels and place in a large bowl. In a shallow bowl, combine the flour, oregano, salt, and pepper. Sprinkle the flour mixture evenly over the lamb and toss to coat. Heat 3 tablespoons of oil in a heavy casserole dish over medium heat. Brown the lamb in batches, adding more oil as needed. Remove lamb and set aside. Add carrots, celery, potatoes, onions, and garlic. Cook, stirring occasionally, 10 minutes until the vegetables start to caramelize. Return lamb to dish. Add wine, bay leaves and lemon peel. Bring to simmer. Cover and place on bottom rack of oven. Cook at 350 degrees 2 hours or until the lamb is very tender.

Yield: 8 to 12 servings

Tortellini Soup

This soup is a feast. Serve with
a crusty loaf of bread and a full bodied red wine.

2 tablespoons olive oil

1 (12-ounce) package smoked kielbasa sausage, thinly sliced

1 onion, chopped

1 cup chopped fennel bulb

4 garlic cloves, minced

1½ tablespoons chopped fresh thyme

½ teaspoon crushed red pepper

10 cups low-salt chicken stock

1 (10-ounce) package frozen chopped spinach, cooked and drained

1 (15-ounce) can great Northern beans, rinsed and drained

1 (9-ounce) package cheese tortellini

1 cup Parmesan cheese

Heat oil in a heavy stockpot. Sauté sausage, onions, fennel, garlic, thyme and red pepper about 12 minutes until vegetables are tender and sausage is browned. Add stock and bring to boil. Stir in spinach and beans. (May be made 1 day in advance.) Cool slightly, cover and refrigerate. Bring to simmer before continuing. Add tortellini. Simmer 5 minutes until pasta is al dente. Ladle into individual bowls. Serve with cheese.

Yield: 9 servings

Strawberry Soup

6 cups strawberries,
hulled and rinsed

1 cup sour cream or
plain yogurt

2 cups orange juice

¼ cup Grand Marnier

Purée all but 12 strawberries in a blender or food processor. Transfer to a large pitcher. Whisk in sour cream, juice and Grand Marnier until well blended. Cover and refrigerate at least 6 hours or overnight. Serve chilled in shallow soup bowls. Slice strawberries lengthwise into ¼-inch slices. Carefully place 3 to 5 slices on top of each serving, making a star pattern.

Yield: 4 to 6 servings

Chilled Cream of Celery Soup

A lovely pale green color, this soup makes a refreshing first course.

3 cups water

3½ cups chopped celery

1 cup chopped onion

½ teaspoon caraway seeds

1 cup buttermilk

salt and pepper to taste

chopped fresh herbs for garnish

Heat water to a simmer. Add celery, onions and caraway seeds. Simmer 30 minutes until tender. Cool. Transfer mixture to a blender. Purée until smooth. Stir in buttermilk, salt and pepper. Refrigerate at least 6 hours or up to 1 day in advance. Serve cold. Garnish with herbs before serving.

Yield: 4 servings

Chilled Carrot, Tomato and Tarragon Soup

This is a very pretty and earthy soup with a lot of flavor.
Try serving in a glass punch cup as an accompaniment
to a main dish salad! Also good served hot!

1 medium onion, minced

4 tablespoons butter

2 pounds carrots, peeled
and diced

2 (16-ounce) cans diced tomatoes
with juice or 3½ cups seeded
and diced fresh tomatoes

3½ cups chicken stock

1 tablespoon chopped fresh
tarragon or 1 teaspoon
dried tarragon

1 cup whipping cream

salt and pepper to taste

finely grated carrots

Sauté onions in butter in a large saucepan until tender. Add carrots and
tomatoes. Stir in stock. Cover and simmer 20 minutes until vegetables are
tender. Add tarragon and simmer 10 minutes more. Transfer mixture to a
blender. Purée until smooth. Add cream, salt and pepper. Chill thoroughly
before serving. Top with tarragon and/or carrots.

Yield: 4 to 6 servings

Artichoke Soup

Serve this one either hot or cold. The taste is delectable.

1 onion, finely chopped
½ cup finely chopped celery
6 tablespoons butter
6 tablespoons all-purpose flour
4 (14-ounce) cans chicken stock
¼ cup lemon juice

1 (8½-ounce) can artichoke
   hearts, drained
¼ teaspoon ground thyme
¼ teaspoon pepper
1 teaspoon salt
2 cups half-and-half
2 egg yolks

Sauté onions and celery in butter until tender. Stir in flour until creamy. Add stock, juice, artichokes, thyme, pepper and salt. Simmer 20 to 30 minutes. Transfer mixture to a blender. Purée until smooth. Add half-and-half. Add egg yolks. Purée again. Transfer back to pot and heat soup over moderate heat, stirring until it barely reaches a boil. Serve warm or cold.

Yield: 4 to 6 servings

Create a menu planner complete with a guest list for future reference. Include ratings for foods served (with the cookbook and page number of recipes rated highly); the beverages served; the date; the theme, if any, the seating arrangement. You can even add photos of the event! It is a great way to avoid duplication when entertaining the same guests and serves as a source to plan a similar event for different guests.

Salads

Kenilworth Train Station

- Kenilworth -

Kenilworth

The newest of the eight Chicago suburban communities fronting on Lake Michigan, Kenilworth is the only North Shore Village developed as a planned community. The first land was purchased by Joseph Sears in 1889. Seven years later, in 1896, the population had reached 300 residents, fulfilling the legal requirement for incorporation. Mr. Sears named the new village Kenilworth, after a delightful trip with his family to Kenilworth, England.

Joseph Sears possessed definite ideas about how a village should be planned. Streets were platted to maximize the availability of sunlight in each home, utilities were placed underground, no alleys or fences were permitted, construction standards were high. A village where family is the foundation should also have a church and school. Mr. Sears gave the land for both.

Kenilworth attracted the attention of many visitors to the Chicago Columbian Exposition in 1893, most notably the Fair's architects and planners. Daniel Burnham designed Sears' home and another residence in Kenilworth, and Franklin Burnham designed the Kenilworth railroad station. Jens Jensen provided landscape planning for many parks and homes in Kenilworth.

The beauty of the village attracted many more distinguished residents, including architect and town planner, George W. Maher. A contemporary and colleague of Frank Lloyd Wright, Maher designed approximately 37 homes in the village. His town planning expertise and civic dedication further enriched the village. The parks and civic sculpture, the entry fountain, stone benches, and planter urns reflect the strong influence of the Arts and Crafts and Prairie styles so prominent in this exclusive community.

An Evening with Friends

Plan to spend an evening with friends on a
chilly fall evening. The trees outside are a full palette of
color and the leaves rustle in the cool breeze. Enjoy conversation
in front of the fireplace - warming both hearts and home.

Skylark Cocktails

Warm Crab and Artichoke Dip

Julienne Salad

Boursin Scalloped Potatoes

Pepper Dijon Flank Steaks

Pumpkin Cheesecake

Chicken Berry Salad

Contributed by Skokie Country Club, Glencoe. Specifically requested by
Tolbert Chisum, President of the Village of Kenilworth.

- POPPY SEED DRESSING -

2 cups sugar	¾ cup cider vinegar
1½ teaspoons salt	¼ cup minced onion
1½ teaspoons dry mustard	2¾ cups canola oil

Beat sugar, salt, mustard, vinegar and onions 20 minutes with an electric
mixer. Slowly add oil and beat another 20 minutes. Pour into an airtight
container and refrigerate. Stores up to 1 month in the refrigerator.

- SALAD -

4 boneless, skinless chicken breast halves	1 cup blue cheese, crumbled
Cajun spices	1 cup toasted walnuts
1½ pints strawberries	4 (8-ounce) packages mesclun greens
2 cups Mandarin orange segments	

Rub chicken with Cajun spice. Sauté chicken in a skillet 5 minutes per side.
Cool and cut each diagonally into 8 pieces. Slice all but 4 strawberries.
Arrange strawberries and oranges in an alternating pattern around rim of
four salad plates. Mound greens in the center. Fan chicken pieces over
greens. Top with walnuts and blue cheese. Drizzle dressing over salad.
Fan remaining 4 strawberries over top.

Yield: 4 servings

Seafood Cobb Salad

Contributed by Metropolitan Club, Chicago. Specifically requested
by Tolbert Chisum, President of the Village of Kenilworth.

Both champagne and balsamic vinaigrettes will complement this salad nicely or
blend the two for a milder flavor. Another tasty option is to mix the following:
1 cup Caesar dressing, 1 cup bleu cheese dressing and ¼ cup red wine vinegar.

1 head romaine or
iceberg lettuce, sliced julienne

1 ounce shrimp, cooked
and chopped

1 ounce snow crabmeat,
cooked and chopped

1 ounce scallops, cooked
and chopped

1 ounce lobster meat, cooked

chopped tomatoes (optional)

salad dressing of choice

Combine lettuce, shrimp, crabmeat, scallops, lobster and tomatoes.
Toss with favorite dressing.

Yield: 2 servings

Julienne Salad

Contributed by Depot Restaurant, Winnetka.

- 1000 ISLAND DRESSING -

mayonnaise and ketchup at 4 to 1 ratio

diced pickles

pinch salt and white pepper

Blend mayonnaise, ketchup, pickles, salt and pepper.

- SALAD -

iceberg lettuce, torn

tomato wedges

cucumber slices

3 ounces ham strips

3 ounces turkey strips

3 ounces Swiss cheese strips

3 ounces American cheese strips

lemon wedges

Combine lettuce, tomatoes, cucumbers, ham, turkey,
Swiss cheese, American cheese and lemons in a large bowl.
Pour dressing over salad and toss to coat.

Yield: 4 servings

Thai Kaffir Lime Chicken Salad

Contributed by Corner Cooks, Winnetka.

- CHICKEN -

4 boneless, skinless chicken breasts halves	5 kaffir lime leaves
	1 cup fish sauce
1 cup soy sauce	1 large piece fresh ginger, chopped

Combine chicken, soy sauce, lime leaves, fish sauce and ginger in a stockpot. Cover with water. Bring just to a boil and turn off heat. Cover and let steep for 1 hour. Remove chicken when cool and reserve liquid. Shred chicken and add a little of the reserved broth to moisten.

- VINAIGRETTE -

½ cup soy sauce	2 tablespoons sesame oil
¼ cup sweet chili sauce	1 tablespoon honey
1 tablespoon minced garlic	1 tablespoon minced ginger
¼ cup fish sauce	1 kaffir lime leaf, julienne
juice of 2 limes	or minced

Whisk together soy sauce, chili sauce, garlic, fish sauce, juice, oil, honey, ginger and lime leaf.

- SALAD -

½ head red cabbage, slivered	1 bunch green onions, julienne
1 (1-pound) package carrots, shredded	½ bunch cilantro, chiffonade cut
	½ bunch basil, chiffonade cut

Combine cabbage, carrots, green onions, cilantro and basil in a large bowl. Add chicken and drizzle with Vinaigrette.

Yield: 4 to 6 servings

Secret Caesar Salad Recipe

Contributed by Tim Smithe on behalf of Walter E. Smithe Custom Furniture.

This is the original recipe that was used in the famous Jim Sain's Restaurant in Chicago in the 1940s. It is shared with the JLE-NS compliments of Smithe Family friends, Richard C. and Barbara Sain Payne of Glenview, Illinois.

Romaine lettuce, about 4 packages or heads

5 garlic cloves

1 cup extra virgin olive oil

4 eggs

3 lemons

1 can flat anchovies

1½ cups Parmesan cheese, freshly grated

1 tablespoon Worcestershire sauce

½ cup croutons

salt and freshly ground black pepper

unfinished, large wooden salad bowl

two large wooden spoons (for tossing the Romaine leaves)

Marinate 5 cloves of garlic in 1 cup olive oil for at least 30 minutes and boil 4 eggs for exactly 1 minute. Drain 1 can of flat anchovies and chop. Rub the garlic cloves into a wooden salad bowl. Place half of the lettuce leaves in the bowl and add ½ of the olive oil and ½ of the Parmesan cheese. Add the rest of the lettuce and remaining cheese, olive oil, lemon juice, and Worcestershire sauce. Add the chopped anchovies and croutons. Sprinkle generously with salt and freshly ground pepper. Toss gently until all leaves are coated in dressing.

Yield: 6 to 8 servings

Easy Chicken Pasta Salad

Contributed by Barbara Rinella, literary
dramatist and academic entertainer, Kenilworth.

1 (12-ounce) package of pasta,
best with mixture of different
pasta shapes

1 medium carrot, shredded

½ cup thinly sliced celery

1 cup honey mustard salad dressing
or honey mustard and wasabi
gourmet dressing

1½ to 2 cups cooked and
cubed chicken

½ medium red onion, sliced thin

½ chopped cup parsley

Prepare pasta according to directions. Drain. Combine pasta, carrots, celery, dressing, chicken, onions and parsley. Toss to coat. Cover and refrigerate at least one hour. Stir gently before serving.

Yield: 6 servings

Zesty Summer Salad

Contributed by Kathy Taslitz Interiors, Northbrook.

This recipe is also wonderful when topped with grilled chicken, shrimp or salmon.

- DRESSING -

¼ cup sugar	1 teaspoon salt
¾ cup olive oil	1 teaspoon fresh squeezed
⅓ cup balsamic vinegar	lime juice

Whisk together sugar, oil, vinegar, salt and lime juice.
Pour dressing into a plastic bottle with a spout top. Cut off about
¼ -inch of the spout top to drizzle dressing on salad.

- SALAD -

8 cups of mixed salad greens	1 cup jicama, chopped and cubed
2 cups of Craisins	
1 large mango, pitted and cubed	Toasted almonds for garnish
½ cup chopped red onion	Thinly sliced lime (with a slit) for garnish
1 tablespoon chopped fresh cilantro	

Combine lettuce, Craisins, mango, onions, cilantro and jicama. Swirl
dressing on individual salad plates. Place salad in the center of plate. Swirl
more dressing on top of salad. Garnish with toasted almonds and lime
slices. Place lime on side of plate for added color.

Yield: 4 to 6 servings

Arugula Salad

An English classic and one of our favorites.

6 cups arugula

½ tablespoon kosher salt

1 tablespoon lemon juice

½ cup Parmigiano-Reggiano cheese (hard)

olive oil

Arrange arugula in a large bowl. Stir in salt and lemon juice.
Grate cheese over salad. Drizzle with olive oil. Serve immediately.

Yield: 4 to 6 servings

Apple and Blue Cheese Tossed Salad

2 Golden Delicious apples, chopped

2 tablespoons lemon juice

4 cups red leaf lettuce

4 cups spinach, torn

½ cup coarsely chopped cashews

½ cup crumbled blue cheese

6 slices bacon, cooked and crumbled

½ cup sliced mushrooms

Red Wine Vinaigrette, page 93

Toss apples with lemon juice. Combine apples, lettuce, spinach, cashews,
blue cheese, bacon and mushrooms. Toss with our Red Wine Vinaigrette.

Yield: 4 servings

Chopped Winter Salad

Missing a few ingredients? Be creative and use what you have.
This is an amazing salad that makes a meal. The dressing is divine and
works wonderfully with most vegetable substitutions.

- DRESSING -

¾ cup olive oil

⅛ teaspoon salt

3 tablespoons lemon juice

½ teaspoon pepper

3 tablespoons sherry wine vinegar

Whisk together oil, lemon juice, vinegar, salt and pepper. Refrigerate until
ready to use. Shake well before adding to salad.

- SALAD -

1 cup dried cranberries

1 cup crumbled
Gorgonzola cheese

1 cup roasted whole pecans

2 Granny Smith apples,
thinly sliced

8 cups mixed salad greens

1 medium red onion, sliced

Combine cranberries, cheese, pecans, apples, mixed greens and onions.
Add other chopped vegetables of your choice. With a large knife or,
preferably, curved knife, chop all ingredients until ingredient is bite size.
Toss with dressing just before serving.

Yield: 4 to 6 servings

Thai Cucumber Salad

Simple, refreshing and a little spicy. We love this salad!
Take it easy on the chilies. Start light and add more for extra flavor.
Gets hot very fast!

1 cup distilled white vinegar

1 cup golden brown or
white sugar

1 teaspoon salt

1 large cucumber

1 to 2 small Thai chilies or ½ to
1 serrano chili, finely chopped

½ cup roasted unsalted peanuts

⅓ cup loosely packed chopped
cilantro, including the stems

Combine vinegar, sugar and salt in a small saucepan and heat over medium heat. Bring to boil, stirring to dissolve the sugar and salt. Cook 1 minute at a gentle boil, stirring occasionally. Remove from heat and cool to room temperature. When ready to serve, peel the cucumber and cut in half lengthwise. Scrape out the seeds. Cut the cucumber crosswise into thin slices. Combine cucumber, chilies, peanuts and cilantro in a mixing bowl. Pour the cooled dressing over salad and mix gently.

Yield: 2 to 4 servings

Pear and Feta Salad
with Apple-Dijon Dressing

Excellent as a light meal or for a heartier meal,
serve along side your favorite grilled chicken.

- APPLE-DIJON DRESSING -

⅓ cup apple cider

⅓ cup honey

½ to ⅔ cup olive oil

2 teaspoons Dijon mustard

1 tablespoon poppy seeds

½ teaspoon salt

Whisk together cider, honey, olive oil, mustard, poppy seeds and salt.
Refrigerate until ready to use.

- SALAD -

2 (10-ounce) packages
lettuce leaves

2 (6-ounce) packages garlic and
herb feta cheese, crumbled

1 cup Craisins

2 Asian pears, sliced

1 cup pecans, toasted

Combine lettuce, cheese, Craisins, pears and pecans.
Toss with dressing just prior to serving.

Yield: 4 servings

Summer Slaw

Perfect for a picnic, a refreshing twist on an old favorite.
Best when made a day in advance to let cabbage soften and let flavors blend.

1 small cabbage, grated

1 bunch parsley, finely chopped

1 (20-ounce) can crushed
pineapple, drained and
reserving juice

3 tablespoons mayonnaise

1 teaspoon sugar

1 teaspoon salt

Combine cabbage, parsley and pineapple. Whisk mayonnaise with small
amount of pineapple juice until smooth. Add sugar and salt.
Stir mayonnaise mixture into cabbage until well coated.

Yield: 6 servings

Perfect Vinaigrette

2 garlic cloves, finely minced

¼ teaspoon sea salt

¼ teaspoon pepper

1 heaping teaspoon Dijon mustard

1 teaspoon honey

1 tablespoon red wine vinegar

3 tablespoons olive oil

Combine garlic, salt, pepper, mustard and honey.
Whisk in vinegar and oil until well blended.

Yield: 2 servings

Red Wine Vinaigrette

Great with any salad, especially the
Apple and Blue Cheese Tossed Salad on page 88.

¼ cup red wine vinegar
⅓ cup vegetable oil
1 teaspoon Worcestershire sauce
1 garlic clove, crushed

½ teaspoon salt
¼ teaspoon dried oregano
2 tablespoons sugar
dash of pepper

Whisk together vinegar, oil,
Worcestershire sauce, garlic, salt, oregano, sugar and pepper.

Yield: 2 servings

House Salad Dressing

A creamy salad dressing. The goat cheese is the secret of its creamy texture.

1 tablespoon Dijon mustard
3 tablespoons white
balsamic vinegar
1 teaspoon lemon pepper

1 tablespoon honey
1 (3-ounce) package goat cheese,
spreadable or room temperature
¾ cup olive oil

Combine mustard, vinegar, pepper,
honey and goat cheese. Slowly whisk in oil.

Yield: 2 to 4 servings

Lemon Ginger Chicken Salad

Love Ginger? It adds flair and dimension to this salad.
Serve in individual pastry shells for bite-size servings.

1 cup mayonnaise

½ cup sour cream

2 tablespoons sugar

1 teaspoon lemon zest

2 tablespoons lemon juice

1 teaspoon ground ginger

½ teaspoon salt

4 cups cooked, cubed chicken

2 cups seedless grapes

½ cup chopped celery

4 cantaloupes or honeydew melon, cut into wedges, remove seeds

slivered almonds, toasted

Combine mayonnaise, sour cream, sugar, zest, lemon juice, ginger, salt, chicken, grapes and celery. Mix until well blended. Spoon mixture into melon wedges. Top with almonds.

Yield: 8 servings

Basil-Chicken-Vegetable Salad

The basil makes this fresh and unique.

1 tablespoon olive oil

1 boneless, skinless chicken breast, halved, cut into ½-inch strips

⅛ cup balsamic vinegar

⅓ cup olive oil

2 tablespoons chopped basil

1 tablespoon capers

½ teaspoon sugar

1 teaspoon salt

1 pound fresh green beans, rinsed and prepared (trim ends and remove strings)

½ teaspoon salt

tomato wedges

basil leaves for garnish

Heat oil in large skillet. Add chicken and cook 5 minutes until tender, stirring often. Set aside. Whisk together vinegar, olive oil, basil, capers, sugar and salt until well blended. Pour dressing over chicken strips. Toss gently. Cover and refrigerate 1 to 2 hours. Pour water to 1-inch depth into a skillet. Add salt and bring to boil. Add beans. Cover and reduce heat. Cook 8 to 10 minutes or until crisp-tender. Drain and plunge into ice cold water to stop cooking process. Arrange beans and tomatoes on salad plates. Top with chicken. Drizzle with dressing and garnish with basil leaves.

Yield: 4 servings

Chicken Salad
with Cranberry French Dressing

Oh, so pretty. Serve at a luncheon and your guests will never forget it.

- CRANBERRY FRENCH DRESSING -

¾ cup vegetable oil   ½ teaspoon paprika

¼ cup vinegar   ¼ teaspoon dry mustard

1 teaspoon salt   1 cup jellied cranberry sauce

1 teaspoon sugar   dash of pepper

Whisk together oil, vinegar, salt, sugar, paprika and mustard.
Beat cranberry sauce until smooth. Gradually blend in oil mixture.
Add pepper to taste.

- SALAD -

4 cups cooked and diced chicken   ½ cup mayonnaise

1 cup chopped celery   ½ cup sour cream

2 cups seedless grapes   lettuce leaves

½ teaspoon salt   salted pecan halves

½ teaspoon pepper   or almonds

Combine chicken, celery, grapes, salt and pepper. Whisk together
mayonnaise and sour cream. Add to chicken mixture. Arrange lettuce
leaves on salad plates. Top with chicken salad. Garnish with pecans or
almonds. Serve with cranberry dressing.

Yield: 6 servings

Spicy Sesame Pasta Salad

What is your favorite shape pasta? Try one of the fun shapes for this dish.
Add chicken or shrimp for a heartier meal.

1 tablespoon olive oil	¼ cup sesame seeds, toasted
pinch of salt	¼ cup chopped green onions
1¼ pounds rotelle pasta	¾ teaspoon garlic powder
¼ cup chopped cilantro	½ teaspoon cayenne pepper
1 cup teriyaki sauce	3 to 4 dashes crushed
¼ cup olive oil	red pepper
¼ cup sesame oil	¼ cup soy sauce

Combine 10 cups water, oil and salt in a large stockpot. Bring to boil.
Add pasta and cook 5 minutes or until al dente. Drain and rinse in cold
water. Drain again. Transfer to a bowl. Add cilantro, teriyaki sauce, olive
and sesame oils, sesame seeds, onions, garlic powder, cayenne,
red pepper and soy sauce. Toss gently. Let stand 30 minutes
or refrigerate overnight. Serve hot or cold.

Yield: 8 servings

Summer Salad

2 tomatoes, cubed	1 (8-ounce) container blue cheese
2 cucumbers, peeled and cubed	or feta cheese, crumbled
1 small onion, diced	Italian dressing to taste (optional)

Combine tomatoes, cucumbers and onions. Refrigerate. Before serving,
add cheese and toss gently. Add dressing.

Yield: 4 servings

Tropical Fruit Salad

A refreshing salad or dessert.

- HONEY ORANGE SAUCE -

⅓ cup unsweetened orange juice

2 tablespoons lemon juice

1½ tablespoons honey

¼ teaspoon ground ginger

dash of ground nutmeg

Whisk together orange juice,
lemon juice, honey, ginger and nutmeg. Refrigerate.

- SALAD -

1 large mango, peeled and diced

2 cups fresh blueberries

2 bananas, sliced

2 cups halved fresh strawberries

2 cups seedless grapes

2 nectarines, peeled and sliced

1 kiwi, peeled and sliced

Combine mango, blueberries, bananas, strawberries,
grapes, nectarines and kiwi in a large bowl. Refrigerate until ready
to serve. Pour sauce over fruit just before serving.

Yield: 10 to 12 servings

Curry Egg Salad

An interesting twist on simple egg salad.
Serve at a tea or as a sandwich on fresh croissants.

6 hard-cooked eggs,
peeled and chopped

1/3 cup mayonnaise

2 tablespoons chopped
mango chutney

1/2 teaspoon curry powder

salt and pepper to taste

white bread slices

Combine eggs, mayonnaise, chutney and curry.
Add salt and pepper. Spread mixture on bread slices.

Yield: 6 servings

To prevent the shells from cracking
when boiling eggs, throw in a lit match.

Vegetables and Sides

Glencoe Historical Society

- Glencoe -

Village of Glencoe

Like many of the North Shore villages, the Potawatomi Indians first walked here. Then in 1835, Anson and Eliza Taylor, with their son, ventured north from the crowds of Chicago to become Glencoe's first non-native family. When the railroad came through in 1855, more pioneers made their way to the area for logging and farming opportunities. Glencoe also became a country escape for wealthy Chicago business owners.

In the center of what was to become the Village of Glencoe, there stood a large stock farm belonging to Matthew Coe, whose daughter married Walter Gurnee, an important figure in early Chicago history. When Gurnee purchased this land from his father-in-law in the mid 1850's, the village, once known as Taylorsport, was renamed Glencoe. Depending on which account you read, the Village of Glencoe got its name from "Coe's Glen", an acknowledgement of Matthew Coe's original ownership of the property in the heart of the town, or Glencoe, Scotland, said to be the homeland of Gurnee's ancestors. Either way, Glencoe's first seal was modeled after the seal of Glencoe, Scotland.

The early village consisted of scattered homes, a small schoolhouse, a church, depot and a couple of stores, loosely connected by dirt roads. People drew their water from wells. Homeowners put up their own oil lamps on posts, where a village lamplighter made regular rounds. In 1869, the newly incorporated Village of Glencoe held some 150 people.

Today, Glencoe boasts a population count of 9000 residents and still maintains the ambiance of a small village by the lakeshore. Poets, statesmen, film actors, film directors, skating champions, generals and captains of industry have either grown up in Glencoe or chosen it as their home. From early pioneers to the movers and shakers of today, Glencoe seems a pretty good place to come from or be going to.

Valentine's Day Dinner

A very special menu for a special guest list of two...or more.

Liquid Gold

Red Pepper Bruschetta

Artichoke Soup

Seared Scallops with Vanilla Sauce over Angel Hair Pasta

Steamed Asparagus with Almond Butter

Baked Pears with Rosemary Maple Custard

Creamed Spinach

Contributed by Glencoe Village President Scott Feldman, on behalf of his wife, Susan, whose family members have lived in the Glencoe area since the 1930's.

3 small or one large onion, chopped

1 tablespoon butter

3 (10-ounce) boxes frozen spinach, partially defrosted

¾ teaspoon salt

1 tablespoon butter

1 tablespoon all-purpose flour

1 cup light sour cream

Worcestershire sauce

Sauté onions in butter until lightly browned. Add spinach and salt. Cover and cook at low heat until the spinach is defrosted. Remove lid and cook at medium heat until liquid evaporates. Purée the spinach mixture in a food processor or with an immersion blender. Melt butter in a saucepan. Whisk in flour. Stir in sour cream until smooth. Add Worcestershire sauce until the mixture becomes tan in color. Add cream sauce to the puréed spinach. Heat thoroughly.

Yield: 6 to 8 serving

The finished creamed spinach may be frozen for future use.

Grilled Tomatoes

Contributed by the Village of Glencoe Public Safety.

4 garden tomatoes	4 basil leaves or
sea salt	thyme, chopped
olive oil	Parmesan cheese to taste

Cut tops off tomatoes. Lightly brush with oil over exposed top.
Sprinkle with sea salt. Sprinkle basil or thyme on top of tomato.
Sprinkle cheese on top. Broil at 400 degrees 5 to 10 minutes.

Yield: 4 servings

Broccoli Soufflé

Contributed by Marian Baird, JLE-NS President 1955-1957.

If you do not like broccoli, try this one. You will love broccoli in a soufflé.

2 (10-ounce) packages frozen chopped broccoli, thawed	1 cup mayonnaise
1 (10¾-ounce) can cream of mushroom soup	1 cup shredded Cheddar cheese
	2 eggs, beaten

Cook broccoli according to package directions. Drain well.
Combine broccoli, soup, mayonnaise, cheese and eggs. Mix well.
Pour mixture into a soufflé dish. Bake at 350 degrees 1 hour.

Yield: 4 to 6 servings

Murray Brothers' Famous Onion Rings

Contributed by the Murray Brothers (Bill, Andy, Ed, Brian, John and Joel).

1 large yellow onion	1 cup panko bread crumbs
2 cups all-purpose flour	1 quart vegetable oil for frying
6 large eggs	salt and pepper to taste
1 cup milk	barbecue sauce
2 cups plain bread crumbs	

Slice onions ½-inch thick. Separate onion rings and place in cold water. Place flour in a shallow pan. Whisk together eggs and milk and pour into another pan. Combine both bread crumbs in a pan. Place onion rings one at a time into flour. Cover entire ring with your dry hand. Place floured onion ring in egg wash and turning onion ring to coat. Place onion ring in bread crumbs and coat thoroughly. Deep fry in 350 degree oil until golden browned. Sprinkle with salt and pepper. Serve with warm barbecue sauce.

Yield: 2 servings

The Murray family grew up in Wilmette, IL. Father, Edward, was a former member and groundskeeper of Indian Hill Golf Club in Winnetka. Sons Ed, Brian and Bill worked as caddies. The collective experience inspired Brian to write the screenplay for the award-winning movie, Caddyshack, which starred his brother, Bill. Borrowing from their success on the big screen along with Andy's professional restaurant experience, the brothers broke culinary ground in the first of a series of Murray Brothers' Caddyshack restaurants.

Spinach Soufflé

Contributed by Roberta Rubin, Bookstall, Winnetka.

9 eggs

2 (10-ounce) packages frozen chopped spinach, thawed and drained

1 (12-ounce) package shredded low-fat Cheddar cheese

1 (12-ounce) package shredded low-fat mozzarella cheese

1 (24-ounce) container low-fat cottage cheese

½ cup plus 1 tablespoon all-purpose flour

¾ cup butter, melted

Beat eggs in a bowl. Add spinach, Cheddar cheese, mozzarella cheese, cottage cheese, flour and butter. Pour mixture into a greased 13 x 9 x 2-inch glass baking dish. Bake at 350 degrees 1 hour. Let stand 10 minutes before serving. The soufflé may be frozen, uncooked. Thaw before cooking.

Yield: 8 to 10 servings

Fresh Cranberry Orange Sauce

Contributed by Lori Andre,
Lori's Designer Shoes, Northfield and Highland Park.

This is a unique and flavorful substitute for traditional cranberry sauce. A great side dish for poultry or pork.

1 mango

1 (12-ounce) package fresh cranberries, uncooked

2 medium navel oranges, quartered, peeled, seeds discarded

⅓ cup honey

Peel mango and cut off as much flesh as possible. Set aside. Chop cranberries in a food processor (not too small). Transfer to a bowl. Chop oranges in processor. Transfer to bowl. Process mango until smooth. Add to cranberry mixture. Stir in honey. For a sweeter taste, add more honey.

Yield: 4 servings

Warm Portobello Mushroom and Asparagus Medley

Contributed by the Old Willow Wine Shoppe, Northbrook.

May be served warm or cold. Great with steaks as a side dish.

- VINAIGRETTE -

1 teaspoon Louisiana hot sauce

3 teaspoons extra virgin olive oil

3 teaspoons balsamic vinegar

½ teaspoon sugar

juice of 1 lime

sea salt and multi-colored peppercorn to taste

Whisk together hot sauce, oil,
vinegar, sugar, juice, salt and pepper. Set aside.

- VEGETABLES -

4 large Portobello mushrooms

1 medium red onion

2 bunches fresh asparagus, trimmed

1 pint cherry tomatoes, halved

goat cheese, crumbled (optional)

Grill mushrooms for 2 to 3 minutes on each side. Immediately remove from heat and cover in a large glass bowl. (The mushrooms will continue to cook.) Grill red onion on both sides 10 minutes until tender. Steam asparagus 3 to 4 minutes until just tender. Slice mushrooms and red onion lengthwise into strips and then cross-wise. Cut asparagus on the diagonal into three equal pieces. Assemble vegetables into a large glass bowl. Toss with vinaigrette. Top with goat cheese.

Yield: 4 to 6 servings

Sweet Baby Ray's Coleslaw

Contributed by Sweet Baby Ray's.

1 cup mayonnaise

½ cup sour cream

2 tablespoons cider vinegar

4 tablespoons sugar

½ teaspoon salt

½ teaspoon pepper

1 cup shredded red cabbage

5 cups shredded green cabbage

3 tablespoons shredded carrots

2 bunches sliced green onions

Whisk together mayonnaise, sour cream, vinegar,
sugar, salt and pepper. Toss with cabbage, carrots and onions.
Let stand until it starts wilting, then refrigerate.

Yield: 4 to 6 servings

Sweet Baby Ray's Baked Beans

Contributed by Sweet Baby Ray's.

4 (28-ounce) cans baked beans

1 (8-ounce) package bacon,
cooked and crumbled

1 yellow onion, diced

1 cup Sweet Baby Ray's
barbecue sauce

3 tablespoons brown sugar

2 tablespoons mustard

½ pound pulled pork

pinch of salt

pinch of pepper

Combine beans, bacon, onions, barbecue sauce, brown sugar, mustard,
pork, salt and pepper in a stockpot. Simmer for 1 hour. Serve warm.

Yield: 8 to 10 servings

Peperoni Alla Piemonte

(Roasted Peppers with Anchovy Sauce)

Contributed by North Shore Community Bank's Customer Celebrity Chef, Nancy Brussat Barocci of Convito Italiano and Betise in Wilmette.

2 pounds red bell peppers	6 tablespoons butter
2 pounds yellow bell peppers	2 tablespoons olive oil
French or Italian bread	3 garlic cloves, finely chopped
2 tablespoons olive oil	6 anchovy fillets, finely chopped
2 cups canned Italian plum tomatoes, drained and chopped	pinch of salt
4 basil leaves, chopped	2 tablespoons capers
salt and pepper to taste	1 tablespoon chopped fresh parsley

Roast peppers under broiler until blackened on all sides. Place immediately into a plastic bag. Seal bag and let peppers sweat 15 minutes. Peel peppers under cold running water. Cut in half, remove seeds and membranes. Dry on paper towels. Cut lengthwise into $\frac{1}{2}$-inch strips. Cut bread into eight $\frac{1}{2}$-inch slices. Toast bread on both sides at 350 degrees until lightly browned. Remove from oven.

Heat oil in a saucepan. Add tomatoes, basil, salt and pepper. Cook over medium heat 20 minutes. Purée mixture in a food processor. Set aside. Melt butter and oil in a skillet. Sauté garlic 1 minute. Remove from heat and add anchovies. Stir with a wooden spoon. Return to heat and cook over low heat until a paste forms. Add salt.

To assemble, place bread rounds in the center of a small gratin dish. Spread 1 tablespoon tomato sauce over bread. Cover bread with pepper strips in alternating fashion, ending by wrapping the strips around the outside of the round. Spread another tablespoon tomato sauce over peppers. Top with 1 tablespoon anchovy mixture. Sprinkle with capers and parsley. Season with salt and pepper. Bake at 350 degree oven 20 to 25 minutes. Serve immediately.

Yield: 8 servings

Asparagus with Gorgonzola Sauce

Select a good quality Gorgonzola cheese
to accompany the asparagus. Sauce can be made in advance.

1 bunch asparagus,
ends trimmed

3 ounces Gorgonzola
cheese, crumbled

juice of 1 lemon

½ cup whipping cream

¼ cup hazelnut or walnut oil

¼ cup virgin olive oil

salt and pepper to taste

½ cup hazelnuts, chopped

Cook asparagus in salted boiling water 4 minutes until crisp-tender.
Drain and plunge into ice water. Pat dry and arrange on a serving tray.
Blend together cheese, juice, cream, hazelnut oil, oil, salt and pepper.
Pour over asparagus and sprinkle with hazelnuts.

Yield: 6 servings

Candles - Put votive containers (glass vases)
upside down on cookie sheet in refrigerator overnight and
the candles will drop out. Always light a new candle for a few
seconds before setting it out for decoration.

Steamed Asparagus with Almond Butter

The perfect way to dress up asparagus with a great balance of flavors.
May substitute fresh green beans for asparagus.

2 tablespoons unsalted butter

3 tablespoons finely chopped shallots

1 large garlic clove, minced

6 tablespoons unsalted butter, softened

3 tablespoons chopped fresh parsley

2 teaspoons fresh lemon juice

2 teaspoons grated lemon zest

salt and pepper to taste

2 pounds asparagus, trimmed

½ cup sliced almonds

Melt 2 tablespoons butter in heavy small skillet over low heat.
Sauté shallots and garlic 5 minutes until tender. Pour into medium bowl.
Blend in six tablespoons butter, parsley, juice and zest. Add salt and
pepper. Steam asparagus until crisp-tender. Melt butter mixture in heavy
large skillet over medium heat. Add almonds and cook 3 minutes until
butter browns, stirring occasionally. Add asparagus and stir until heated
through. Add salt and pepper. Divide asparagus among plates.

Yield: 8 servings

After steaming vegetables, let the water cool
and pour over your plants. It conserves water and
your plants will love the extra nutrients.

Roasted Corn Salad

Fresh corn is a Midwest staple. This recipe is great with our local seasonal corn.

3 cups fresh corn kernels,
about 5 ears
1 teaspoon vegetable oil
2 tablespoons white
balsamic vinegar
2 teaspoons vegetable oil
1 tablespoon Dijon mustard

¼ teaspoon salt
¼ teaspoon black pepper
1 cup chopped seeded tomato
½ cup chopped sweet
red bell pepper
½ cup chopped green onions

Combine corn and 1 teaspoon oil in a greased baking dish. Bake at 425 for 20 minutes or until browned, stirring occasionally. Mix together vinegar, oil, mustard, salt and pepper in a medium bowl. Stir in corn. Add tomatoes, peppers and onions. Mix well. Serve warm or at room temperature.

Yield: 4 servings

When cooking corn on the cob, add a cup of milk to the water. This makes the corn delicious and sweet.

Garden of Eden Vegetables

This requires some serious chopping, but well worth the effort.
It is even better the next day. Great for a crowd.

1 cup olive oil

2 garlic cloves, minced

1/8 cup minced parsley

1 teaspoon crumbled bay leaf

1 tablespoon ground thyme

1 teaspoon ground marjoram

1 1/4 tablespoons salt

1/4 teaspoon crushed red pepper

1 eggplant, unpeeled and cubed

1 zucchini, cut into
1/2-inch thick slices

1 sweet red bell pepper,
cut into 1-inch cubes

1 large onion, sliced

1/2 cup sliced celery

1 cup shredded cabbage

1 cup 2-inch cut green beans

1/2 cup sliced carrots

1/2 small cauliflower,
broken into small florets

2 medium tomatoes, sliced

1/4 pound seedless grapes

1/4 cup peas

salt to taste

Whisk together oil, garlic, parsley, bay leaf, thyme, marjoram,
salt and red pepper. Arrange eggplant in a greased casserole dish. Layer
the zucchini, peppers, onions, celery, cabbage, green beans, carrots and
cauliflower. Sprinkle each layer with oil mixture except for the tomatoes,
grapes and peas. Cover and bake at 350 degrees 1 hour. Top with a
layer of tomatoes, grapes and peas. Sprinkle with salt. Cover and
bake an additional 15 minutes.

Yield: 6 servings

Lemon Tarragon Green Beans

Simply put, a beautiful, light and delicious way to enhance fresh beans.

2 pounds green beans, trimmed

2 tablespoons extra virgin olive oil

2 tablespoons lemon juice or to taste

2 tablespoons finely chopped tarragon or to taste

salt and pepper to taste

tarragon sprigs for garnish

Cooking in two batches, blanch beans in salted boiling water 2 to 3 minutes or until crisp-tender. Plunge beans into ice water. Drain beans and pat dry. May cover and refrigerate at this point. Just before serving, toss beans, oil, juice, tarragon, salt and pepper. Garnish with tarragon sprigs.

Yield: 8 servings

Green Beans with Feta and Pecans

The nuts and cheese add a new dimension to green beans.

1/3 cup white vinegar

1/2 teaspoon minced garlic

1 teaspoon dill

1/4 teaspoon salt

1/4 teaspoon freshly ground pepper

2/3 cup olive oil

2 pounds green beans, trimmed and cut into 1-inch pieces

1/2 cup chopped red onion

1 cup crumbled feta cheese

1 cup pecans, toasted and coarsely chopped

Combine vinegar, garlic, dill, salt and pepper. Whisk in oil. Cook beans just until crisp-tender. Drain and plunge into cold water. Drain and pat dry. Place in a shallow serving bowl. Sprinkle with onions, cheese and pecans. Just before serving, add oil mixture and toss gently until well coated.

Yield: 4 to 6 servings

Boursin Scalloped Potatoes

2 cups heavy cream
1 (15-ounce) package Boursin
cheese with herbs

1 (8-ounce) package cream cheese
3 pounds small red potatoes,
peeled and thinly sliced
salt and pepper to taste

Heat cream in a saucepan. Add Boursin and cream cheese. Cook and stir
until cheese melts and is smooth and bubbly (not boiling). Remove from
heat. Pour small amount in the bottom of a greased 13 x 9 x 2-inch baking
dish. Arrange a layer of potatoes in an overlapping pattern over sauce.
Sprinkle with salt and pepper. Pour some sauce over potatoes.
Repeat layering potatoes and sauce. Bake at 400 degrees 1 hour
or until golden browned and tender. Serve hot.

Yield: 8 servings

Greek Potatoes

2 teaspoons kosher salt
1½ pounds new potatoes, halved
4 tablespoons olive oil
½ cup pitted and sliced
Kalamata or oil-cured olives

¼ cup chopped fresh mint
½ teaspoon freshly
ground black pepper
1 teaspoon lemon zest
1 teaspoon kosher salt

Combine salt and 3 quarts of water in a stockpot.
Add potatoes and bring to boil. Cook 20 to 25 minutes or until tender.
Drain well. Heat oil in a large skillet over medium-high heat. Add potatoes
and toss to coat. Cook 5 minutes per side until golden browned.
Stir in olives and mint. Add pepper, zest and salt.

Yield: 6 servings

Most Excellent Twice Baked Potatoes

6 baking potatoes

1 (8-ounce) container sour cream

1 cup shredded Cheddar cheese

2 green onions, chopped

1 tablespoon snipped parsley

salt to taste

2 tablespoons butter, softened

¼ cup milk

2 tablespoons melted butter

Bake potatoes at 400 degrees 1 hour. Cool 10 minutes. Cut a ¼-inch slice off the top of potatoes. Carefully scoop out the pulp. Mash pulp in a bowl. Add sour cream, cheese, onions, parsley, salt, butter and milk. Beat until smooth. Spoon mixture back into potato shells. Brush with butter. May be refrigerated at this point. Bake at 400 degrees 20 to 25 minutes.

Yield: 6 servings

Put made-ahead mashed potatoes
covered with plastic wrap over a pot of boiling water
to keep them warm until serving time.

Redskin Potato Salad

Fry any leftovers the next morning and
serve with your favorite eggs for a yummy breakfast.

3½ pounds redskin potatoes, sliced

⅓ cup chopped shallots
or green onions

¼ cup dry white wine

3 tablespoons Dijon mustard

2 tablespoons canola or
vegetable oil

½ teaspoon pepper

½ cup fresh parsley

crumbled blue cheese

Cook potatoes in salted boiling water 10 to 15 minutes until fork tender.
Cool under running water and drain. Slice potatoes and place in large
serving bowl. Add shallots. Whisk together wine, mustard, oil and pepper.
Pour mixture over potatoes and toss gently. Add parsley and toss again.
Serve warm or at room temperature with blue cheese
on the side or sprinkled on top.

Yield: 6 to 8 servings

Traditional Southern Sweet Potatoes

Gorgeous fall flavors and color.

4 large sweet potatoes
½ cup packed brown sugar
½ cup heavy cream
1 teaspoon cinnamon
½ teaspoon grated nutmeg
1 teaspoon vanilla

1 tablespoon orange zest
2 tablespoons fresh squeezed orange juice
½ cup butter, melted
1 cup pecan pieces
mini marshmallows

Bake sweet potatoes at 350 degrees 30 minutes or until soft. In a large bowl, combine brown sugar, cream, cinnamon, nutmeg, vanilla, zest, juice, butter and pecans. Remove pulp from potato skins and add to mixture. Spoon mixture into a soufflé dish. Top with marshmallows. Bake at 350 degrees 30 minutes or until marshmallows are slightly browned.

Yield: 4 servings

The inventor of EKCO cookware,
Edward Keating, comes from Glencoe, IL.

Blue Cheese Potato Salad

Tell everyone you will bring the potato salad
and surprise them with this classed up version. Delish!

8 redskin potatoes

2 tablespoons chopped parsley

3 green onions with tops, chopped

2½ teaspoons salt

1 cup sour cream

½ cup slivered almonds, toasted

¼ teaspoon white pepper

8 ounces blue cheese

¼ cup white wine vinegar

3 hard-cooked eggs, sliced

cooked and crumbled bacon for garnish (optional)

Boil potatoes until tender. Peel potatoes while warm. Cool and dice.
Add parsley, onions, salt, sour cream, almonds, pepper,
cheese, vinegar and eggs. Garnish with bacon.

Yield: 6 servings

Spinach and Artichoke Casserole

1 medium onion, chopped

¼ cup butter

2 (10-ounce) packages frozen chopped spinach, thawed and squeezed dry

2 cups sour cream

¼ cup grated Parmesan cheese

1 (14-ounce) can artichoke hearts, drained and chopped

salt and pepper to taste

Sauté onions in butter until soft. Stir in spinach, sour cream, cheese,
artichokes, salt and pepper. Spoon mixture into a 9 x 9 x 2-inch square
baking dish. Bake at 325 degrees 25 minutes or until bubbly.

Yield: 4 to 6 servings

Summer Strata

A great way to use homegrown vegetables.

1½ to 2 pounds yellow squash, sliced ¼ to ½-inch thick

1 to 2 large sweet onions preferably Vidalia, sliced ¼ to ½-inch thick

¼ cup butter, cut into pieces

1 cup Parmesan cheese

2 to 3 large ripe tomatoes, sliced ¼ to ½-inch thick

salt and pepper to taste

Parmesan cheese for garnish

Arrange squash in the bottom of a greased 13 x 9 x 2-inch baking dish. Top with a layer of onions. Dot with butter. Sprinkle half the cheese. Place a layer tomatoes on top. Sprinkle with salt and pepper. Repeat layers. Cover and bake at 350 degrees 20 to 30 minutes. Uncover and top with more cheese. Bake an additional 10 minutes. Serve hot.

Yield: 8 to 10 servings

Zucchini Soufflé

½ yellow or sweet onion, chopped

2 tablespoons olive oil

3 cups grated zucchini

1 cup all-purpose flour

⅓ pound provolone cheese, shredded

3 eggs, beaten

¼ cup vegetable oil

3 tablespoons Parmesan cheese

2 teaspoons chopped basil

1 teaspoon baking powder

1 teaspoon salt

½ teaspoon pepper

1 tablespoon Parmesan cheese

Sauté onions in oil until tender. Combine onions, zucchini, flour, provolone cheese, eggs, oil, Parmesan cheese, basil, baking powder, salt and pepper. Spoon mixture into a greased 10-inch glass or metal pie plate or 12-inch square, rectangle or oval baking dish. Bake at 350 degrees 50 minutes or until golden browned. Sprinkle with Parmesan cheese. Cool 15 minutes before slicing.

Yield: 6 to 8 servings

Pasta

Schmidt Burnham Log House

- Winnetka -

Winnetka

In 1836, Erastus and Zeruah Patterson were passing through the area on their way from Vermont to Wisconsin. So taken with its beauty (present-day Lloyd Park), they settled with their children and established the Patterson Tavern, a place for people to stop along the Green Bay Trail. Winnetka's first business!

Eighteen years later, in anticipation of the railroad, Charles Peck and Walter Gurnee, platted three hundred acres in New Trier Township along the shores of Lake Michigan. Sarah Peck, Charles' wife, named the land Winnetka, a Native American word thought to mean "beautiful land." In 1869, Winnetka was incorporated as a village.

In 1933, a ten-year project began under the leadership of Harold L. Ickes, a Winnetka resident and Secretary of the Interior under Franklin Roosevelt. The project, to develop Skokie Lagoons, made the former lake bay into an eco-friendly lagoon. Today, it's fully stocked with fish such as northern pike, carp, walleye, and catfish. Imagine family picnics and fishing excursions and you'll get a picture of what it's like along our treasured lagoon.

Winnetka's child centered approach to education is due in great part to the work and vision of Carleton Washburne, Winnetka Superintendent from 1919 to 1943. In his "Winnetka Plan" of education, Washburne advocated individualized curriculum materials and the celebration of each child's learning style and interests. Developing a model of education, Washburne's plan continues to receive worldwide recognition.

With over 12,000 residents, Winnetka continues to be a progressive village modeled after the sense of community and family that was so important to its founders.

Lunch with the Girls

Surrounded by friends...a fun drink...a light lunch...
followed by chocolate. It's all good.

Pear Martinis with Lemon and Rosemary

Curry Pâté

Cream of Celery Soup

Zucchini Bread

Chicken Salad with Cranberry French Dressing

Cappuccino Brownies

Summer's Day Pasta

Contributed by Winnetka President, Ed Woodbury.

6 ounces Parmesan cheese,
cut into tiny squares

2 cups fresh basil,
cut into thin strips

3/4 cup pine nuts,
lightly toasted

3 garlic cloves, finely diced
(or more to taste)

1½ cups olive oil

salt and freshly ground pepper

1 pound linguine

cherry tomato halves

Combine cheese, basil, nuts, garlic, oil, salt and pepper. Let stand at room temperature for 3 hours. Cook linguine until al dente. Drain and toss immediately with cheese mixture. Serve warm or at room temperature on a platter with tomatoes placed around the edge.

Yield: 3 to 4 servings

Favorite Linguine Carbonara

Contributed by the Winnetka Historical Society.

¼ pound shredded lean prosciutto

4 garlic cloves, minced

2 tablespoons butter

3 eggs

1 cup whipping cream

salt and pepper to taste

1 pound linguine pasta, cooked al dente

Parmesan cheese

Sauté prosciutto and garlic in butter until browned. In a small bowl, beat together eggs, cream, salt and pepper. Add pasta to prosciutto and stir well. Add cream mixture. Cook and stir vigorously 3 minutes until eggs are cooked. Serve immediately with Parmesan cheese.

Yield: 4 to 6 servings

For a great buffet, set up a good traffic pattern so guests are comfortable maneuvering around the food. For a large group, consider setting the buffet table with duplicate dishes on each side so dinner guests may serve themselves from either side. Consider place cards describing foods or beverages - it keeps the buffet line moving.

Seared Scallops with Vanilla Sauce over Angel Hair Pasta

Contributed by Nielsen-Massey Vanillas, Inc.

1 stick butter

½ pound sea scallops

2 tablespoons minced onion

1 garlic clove, minced

1 cup heavy cream

½ teaspoon Nielsen-Massey Madagascar Bourbon Pure Vanilla Extract

½ pound angel hair pasta, cooked al dente

chopped parsley for garnish

Melt butter in a 12-inch skillet. Add scallops and cook 1 minute per side just until done. Remove from pan and keep warm. Add onions and garlic and sauté 2 minutes. Stir cream and vanilla. Cook and stir over medium heat until slightly thickened. Return scallops to pan and stir to coat. Serve over pasta. Sprinkle with parsley.

Yield: 2 servings

Spaghetti Carbonara

Contributed by Dave's Italian Kitchen, Evanston.

2 tablespoons olive oil
¾ pound bacon, chopped
½ cup chopped onion
12 ounces spaghetti, cooked al dente

3 eggs
1¼ cups whipping cream
¼ cup Parmesan cheese
salt and pepper to taste

Heat oil in a large skillet over medium heat. Add bacon and sauté until just beginning to brown, about 4 minutes. Add onions and sauté until translucent, about 4 minutes. Drain oil from skillet. Whisk together eggs, cream and cheese. Add spaghetti and toss to coat. Transfer mixture to skillet with bacon and onions. Cook over low heat until mixture thickens and is heated thoroughly, stirring frequently. Do not boil. Add salt and pepper. Divide among individual plates. Serve with Parmesan cheese.

Yield: 4 servings

Bill Carmody's Pesto

Contributed by Bill Carmody, Head Basketball
Coach at Northwestern University, Evanston.

2 bunches (approximately 6 cups) fresh basil

¼ pound Parmesan cheese, cubed

¼ pound pecorino cheese, cubed

¼ cup pine nuts

⅓ cup walnuts

1 clove garlic, peeled

1 cup cold salted butter, cubed

3 tablespoons cream cheese

¾ cup good quality olive oil

¼ cup heavy cream

fresh ground pepper, to taste

Remove stems from basil; rinse leaves and pat dry. Set aside. Add Parmesan and pecorino cheeses to bowl of food processor and process until completely grated. Add pine nuts, walnuts and garlic and process for an additional 30 seconds. Add basil and pulse until leaves are completely chopped. Remove processor lid and add butter pieces and cream cheese to basil mixture. Return lid and process until smooth. Combine olive oil and heavy cream in measuring cup and in a slow, steady stream pour mixture into running processor, blending completely until thick and creamy. Add pepper to taste.

Wild Mushroom Pasta

Contributed by Lori Andre, Lori's Designer Shoes,
Northfield and Highland Park.

May use shiitake, oyster, morel or chanterelles
or any combination of wild mushrooms.

1½ pounds brown or white mushrooms, sliced

6 cups stock, beef, chicken or vegetable

1 tablespoon butter

¼ cup good olive oil

1 large shallot, minced

2 garlic cloves, minced

1½ pounds assorted wild mushrooms, cleaned and sliced

salt and pepper to taste

chopped thyme

1 pound gemelli or penne pasta, cooked al dente

chopped parsley and shaved Parmesan cheese for garnish

Combine mushrooms and stock in a 6-quart stockpot. Boil down until you have approximately 3 cups of stock. Using a slotted spoon, remove mushrooms and discard. Set stock aside. Heat a large sauté pan with butter and oil over medium heat. Sauté shallots, garlic, wild mushrooms, salt and pepper approximately 15 minutes. Reduce to low heat. Slowly add mushroom stock, half cup at a time, until liquid is absorbed. Add thyme and continue to add stock until almost absorbed. Pour mushroom sauce over pasta. Top with parsley and Parmesan cheese.

Yield: 4 to 6 servings

Country Rigatoni

2 pounds Italian sausage,
1 pound regular and
1 pound spicy or hot

1 (48-ounce) can high quality
marinara sauce

1 pint heavy cream

5 to 6 ounces fresh
Parmesan cheese

2 (8-ounce) packages
rigatoni pasta

Peel casing from sausage. Brown and break apart in a deep skillet.
Drain fat. Add sauce and bring to a simmer. Add cream and stir well,
keeping a low simmer so the sauce is barley bubbling. Grate cheese into
sauce. Stir and keep warm. This will thicken the sauce. Meanwhile, cook
pasta until al dente. Drain and pour pasta into sauce.
Toss to coat and serve immediately.

Yield: 8 servings

Old Italian Rule-The sauce should always wait for the pasta.
The pasta should never wait for the sauce. Always serve pasta
immediately after cooking. Also, never rinse pasta when serving with
warm sauces. Rinsing will wash away the natural starches
that allow the sauce to adhere to the pasta.

Asparagus Risotto
with Shiitake Mushrooms

Try this recipe the next time you are entertaining.
Perfect enough for a very special occasion.

4 cups chicken stock
1 large bunch asparagus
¼ cup extra virgin olive oil
2 cups sliced shiitake mushrooms
salt and pepper to taste
1 cup finely chopped onions
1 tablespoon minced garlic
1 cup Arborio rice
½ cup dry white wine

1½ teaspoons finely chopped thyme
1 tablespoon unsalted butter
¾ cup Parmesan cheese
1½ tablespoons finely chopped flat leaf parsley
1½ teaspoons lemon zest (optional)
Parmesan cheese

Bring stock to boil. Separate cut tops from stems of asparagus.
Add stems to stock. Reduce heat and simmer 7 minutes, until stems are
tender. Remove stems and throw away. Slice the tops of asparagus on a
diagonal into ¼-inch thick pieces. Set aside. Heat oil in a large stockpot
until hot. Add mushrooms and cook 1 minute, without stirring. Add salt and
pepper. Cook 5 minutes more. Set aside. Reduce heat and add onions.
Cook 2 minutes until soft and translucent. Stir in garlic and cook 1 minute.
Add rice and stir until the grains look pearly white, about 4 minutes. Add
wine and cook until pot is nearly dry. Add ½ cup stock. Stir and cook
until absorbed. Continue adding stock, ½ cup at a time, until all liquid is
absorbed, 18 minutes until rice is almost cooked. Stir in thyme mushrooms
and asparagus tips. Cook 5 minutes more until asparagus is tender.
Remove from heat. Stir in butter, cheese, parsley and zest.
Serve with Parmesan cheese.

Yield: 4 to 6 servings

Chicken and Smoked Ham Lasagna

Rich and tasty.

¼ cup butter

1 medium onion, chopped

1 garlic clove, minced

⅓ cup all-purpose flour

⅛ teaspoon pepper

1½ cups chicken stock

½ cup white wine

1 cup milk

1 (16-ounce) package lasagna noodles, cooked al dente

2 cups cooked and cubed chicken

1 (8-ounce) package shredded mozzarella cheese

1 (8-ounce) package shredded provolone cheese

6 oz. thinly sliced smoked ham or prosciutto

1 (10-ounce) package frozen chopped spinach, thawed and drained

½ cup mushrooms, sliced and sautéed in 1 tablespoon butter

½ cup Romano cheese

½ cup Parmesan cheese

In a saucepan, melt butter. Sauté onions and garlic until tender but not browned. Whisk in flour and pepper. Add stock, wine and milk. Cook until thick and bubbly. Spoon one-fourth sauce into a 13 x 9 x 2-inch baking dish. Layer noodles, chicken, half mozzarella, half provolone, half ham and one-third sauce. Top with another layer of noodles, then spinach, mushrooms, remaining mozzarella, remaining provolone, remaining ham and one-third sauce. Layer with remaining noodles. Pour remaining sauce on top. Sprinkle Parmesan and Romano cheese over top. Bake at 350 degrees 40 to 45 minutes or until thoroughly heated. Let stand 10 minutes before cutting and serving.

Yield: 6 to 8 servings

Farfalle with Pesto and Tomatoes

*There is nothing better than fresh pesto
made from basil out of your own garden.*

3 cups packed basil leaves

½ cup plus 2 tablespoons olive oil

⅓ cup pine nuts

3 large garlic cloves, chopped

¾ cup Parmesan cheese

salt and pepper to taste

1½ pounds farfalle pasta

3 cups chopped, seeded
   plum tomatoes or
   2 (14½-ounce) cans
   diced tomatoes, drained

½ cup Parmesan cheese

Combine basil, oil, nuts and garlic in a food processor. Blend until smooth. Transfer to a small bowl. Add cheese, salt and pepper. (May be made one day in advance. Cover surface with oil. Cover and refrigerate. Remove top oil layer before using.) Cook pasta in boiling water until al dente. Drain pasta, reserving ½ cup cooking liquid. Return pasta to pot. Add 1 cup pesto and reserved cooking liquid. Toss to blend. Stir in tomatoes. Transfer to serving bowl. Sprinkle with cheese. Serve immediately.

Yield: 8 servings

Penne with Sausage, Wild Mushrooms and Spinach

3 tablespoons olive oil

¾ pound pork, chicken or turkey sausages, sliced thick

¾ pound mushrooms, sliced thick

¾ cup chopped onions or shallots

5 garlic cloves, minced

½ teaspoon cayenne pepper

1 (10-ounce) package fresh or frozen spinach, cooked and drained

1¼ cups chicken stock or 2 bouillon cubes and 1¼ cups water

1 (16-ounce) package penne or other pasta, cooked al dente

2 cups shredded provolone or mozzarella cheese

Heat oil in large stockpot. Brown sausage. Add mushrooms, onions, garlic and cayenne. Sauté 10 minutes. Add spinach and stock. Cook 2 minutes or until spinach wilts. Add pasta and cheese. Toss until cheese melts.

Yield: 4 to 6 servings

Penne with Asparagus and Basil

A great recipe for fresh seasonal asparagus.

4 garlic cloves, minced

pinch of crushed red pepper

2 tablespoons olive oil

1 pound asparagus, cut
into ½-inch lengths or
1 (10-ounce) package frozen
cut asparagus, thawed

4 tomatoes, seeded and chopped

1 cup chicken stock or 1 bouillon
and 1 cup water

¼ cup thinly sliced basil or
2 teaspoons dried

salt and pepper to taste

8 ounces penne pasta,
cooked al dente

⅔ cup Parmesan cheese

¼ cup chopped parsley or
2 teaspoons dried

¼ cup finely chopped basil or
2 teaspoons dried

Sauté garlic and red pepper in oil 2 minutes until garlic is golden browned.
Add asparagus, tomatoes, stock and basil. Cook 8 minutes until asparagus
is crisp-tender. Add salt and pepper. Remove from heat. Pour sauce over
pasta. Add cheese, parsley and basil. Toss to coat and serve.

Yield: 4 servings

Pasta with Sausage and Chicken

2 skinless, boneless chicken breast halves, cut into 1-inch pieces

3 tablespoons olive oil

½ cup dry white wine

1 pound hot Italian sausage, casing removed

2 cups chopped onions

1 red bell pepper, julienne cut

1 (14½-ounce) can diced tomatoes in juice

1¼ cups chicken stock

2 tablespoons tomato paste

1 tablespoon chopped garlic

1 tablespoon chopped rosemary or 2 teaspoons dried

12 ounces pasta of choice, cooked al dente

1½ cups Parmesan cheese

¼ cup chopped parsley or 1 tablespoon dried (optional)

Sauté chicken in oil 5 minutes. Using a slotted spoon, transfer chicken to a bowl. Add wine to skillet. Boil 3 minutes, scraping up browned bits, until reduced to 2 tablespoons. Pour wine over chicken. Add sausage, onions and peppers to same skillet. Cook 10 minutes, breaking up sausage with back of spoon. Mix in tomatoes, stock, tomato paste, garlic and rosemary. Simmer 10 minutes until reach sauce consistency. Return chicken and juices. Stir to heat thoroughly. Add cooked pasta, 1 cup cheese and parsley. Transfer to a large bowl and toss to coat. Serve with remaining cheese.

Yield: 4 servings

Not Your Ordinary Mac and Cheese

Delicious!

kosher salt

vegetable oil

8 ounces elbow macaroni

2 cups milk

2 tablespoons butter

2 tablespoons truffle oil

¼ cup all-purpose flour

2 cups shredded Gruyère cheese

2 cups shredded Swiss cheese

¼ teaspoon freshly ground pepper

¼ teaspoon ground nutmeg

¾ cup white bread crumbs

Parmesan cheese

Bring salted water to boil. Add vegetable oil and pasta. Cook until pasta is al dente. Drain and set aside. Heat milk until hot but not boiling. Set aside. Melt butter in a 2-quart saucepan. Over low heat, whisk in truffle oil and flour and cook 2 minutes until smooth. Slowly whisk in hot milk. Cook 1 to 2 minutes until smooth and thickened. Remove from heat. Combine sauce, Gruyère cheese, Swiss cheese, pepper, nutmeg and pasta. Stir well. Pour mixture into a 2-quart baking dish. Top with bread crumbs. Sprinkle with Parmesan cheese. Bake at 375 degrees 30 to 35 minutes until bubbly and golden brown.

Yield: 6 servings

Penne alla Vodka

Guests who enjoy garlic and spice will love this dish!

1 pound penne pasta

¼ cup extra virgin olive oil

10 garlic cloves, crushed

35 ounces crushed tomatoes

salt, pepper and crushed red pepper to taste

¼ cup vodka

½ cup heavy cream

2 tablespoons unsalted butter or olive oil

2-3 tablespoons chopped fresh Italian parsley

¾ cup freshly grated high quality Parmesan cheese plus more for passing

Bring 6 quarts salted water to a boil in an 8-quart pot over high heat. Add pasta. Return to boil. Cook the pasta partially covered, stirring occasionally, 8 to 10 minutes until done. Meanwhile heat the olive oil in a large skillet over medium heat. Sauté garlic 3 minutes until slightly browned. Carefully add tomatoes. (They will splatter.) Bring to boil. Add salt and crushed red pepper. Boil 2 minutes. Pour in vodka. Reduce heat and simmer until the pasta is ready. Just before the pasta is done, remove garlic from sauce. Add cream. Add butter and swirl skillet to incorporate into sauce. Drain the pasta, return to pot and pour in sauce. Bring to boil, stirring to coat the pasta with sauce. Add more salt and pepper to taste. Sprinkle parsley over the pasta and heat until sauce is reduced and clings to pasta. Remove from heat. Add cheese and toss to coat.
Serve immediately, passing additional cheese.

Yield: 4 to 6 servings

White Lasagna

A rich and hearty dish that makes lasagna an elegant affair.

1 pound ground beef
1 pound hot Italian sausage
1 cup finely chopped celery
3/4 cup finely chopped onion
1 garlic clove, minced
2 teaspoons dried basil, crushed
1 teaspoon dried oregano, crushed
1/2 teaspoon Italian herb seasoning
salt and pepper to taste
1 cup half-and-half

1 (3-ounce) package cream cheese, cubed
1/2 cup dry white wine
2 cups shredded Cheddar cheese
1 1/2 cups shredded Gouda cheese
1 (12-ounce) container cottage cheese
1 egg, slightly beaten
8 ounces lasagna noodles, cooked al dente
1 (12-ounce) package sliced mozzarella cheese

Cook ground beef, sausage, celery, onions and garlic until meat is browned and vegetables are tender. Drain fat. Stir in basil, oregano, Italian seasonings, salt and pepper. Add half-and-half and cream cheese. Stir over low heat until cheese melts. Stir in wine and gradually add Cheddar and Gouda cheeses. Stir over low heat until cheese is nearly melted. Remove from heat. In a separate bowl, blend cottage cheese and egg. To assemble, layer noodles in a 13 x 9 x 2-inch baking dish. Spoon half of meat mixture, half of mozzarella slices and half cottage cheese mixture. Repeat layers. Bake uncovered at 375 degrees 30 minutes. Let stand for 10 minutes before serving.

Yield: 6 servings

Linguine with Artichoke-Walnut Sauce

The nuts give this a delicate earthy taste. For even more flavor,
try adding olives and lemon zest just before serving!

1 to 1½ garlic cloves, minced

¼ teaspoon crushed red pepper

3 tablespoons olive oil

½ cup walnut pieces, toasted

1 (12-ounce) jar marinated artichoke hearts, drained, rinsed and coarsely chopped

¼ cup Parmesan cheese

½ teaspoon salt

¼ teaspoon freshly ground pepper

8 ounces spinach linguine

Sauté garlic and red pepper in oil. Cool garlic mixture. Combine garlic mixture, walnuts, artichokes, cheese, salt and pepper in a large bowl. Cook pasta al dente, drain and immediately toss with walnut mixture.

Yield: 4 to 6 servings

Entrées

One of many beautiful walking trails in Northfield

- Northfield -

Northfield

Northfield is a small, seventy five year old village nestled between Winnetka and Northbrook. Thanks to its hometown charm and countryside atmosphere, Northfield is consistently rated as one of the North Shore's best places to live. With a population of just under 6000, Northfield residents pride themselves on sharing a strong community spirit.

First incorporated in 1927, the village of Northfield made a commitment to protect their wide open spaces. Continuing today, this is seen with the balance between the rural atmosphere and modern commercial development. Many of the properties in Northfield are over an acre and set on tree lined country lanes, and some residents keep horses and even chickens.

Once called "River Folks" by the residents of Winnetka and Wilmette, the original settlers of Northfield had to ride their wagons across the Skokie Lagoons and the north branch of the Chicago River. The area was first settled by John Happ, a German immigrant who moved into the area from neighboring Winnetka. Moving his family of ten children and his popular blacksmith shop to the rural area created a pull for other families to move to the countryside.

In the early 1920s, the community changed dramatically when a powerful Chicago entrepreneur, Samuel Insull, built the Skokie Valley Line of the North Shore Railway. With this vital development, he held a contest to name the Village. "Wau-Bun" an Indian word meaning "Dawn" and the name of a Potawatomi Indian Chief, was the winner. Soon, however, the name fell out of popularity. In 1927, Wau-Bun was formally dropped in favor of Northfield, referring to the community's location from Chicago.

Growing at a leisurely pace through the remainder of the century, the Village developed into a vibrant community. With its colorful history, pastoral charm and friendly tone, the "River Folks" of the North Shore take great pleasure and pride in their beautiful little village of Northfield.

Holiday Buffet

This elegant affair is one that
will be talked about for holidays to come.

Cranberry Margaritas

Holiday Egg Nog

Spiced Nuts

Holiday Cheese Puffs

Old World Brisket

Zucchini Soufflé

Traditional Southern Sweet Potatoes

Chopped Winter Salad

Italian Cream Cake

Mincemeat Cream Cheese Pie

Cranberry Pistachio Biscotti

Pepper Dijon Flank Steaks

Contributed by John C. Birkinbine, Jr. President of Northfield.

1 cup olive oil
½ cup red wine vinegar
½ cup Dijon mustard
1 tablespoon coarsely
ground pepper
1 tablespoon minced thyme

1 tablespoon minced
rosemary
3 flank steaks, about
1¼-pound each
thyme and rosemary
sprigs for garnish

Whisk together oil, vinegar, mustard, pepper, thyme and rosemary.
Place steaks in a large zip-top plastic bag. Pour in marinade and turn to
coat. Refrigerate at least 4 hours. Place steaks on grill. Season with pepper.
Grill 5 minutes per side for medium rare. To serve, thinly slice steaks
on diagonal across the grain. Arrange slices on a platter and
garnish with thyme and rosemary sprigs.

Yield: 8 servings

Use freshly ground pepper.
Use coarse salt on beef (especially the finer cuts).

Cottage Pie

Contributed by Lady Margaret Thatcher, former British Prime Minister.
There is a version of this recipe with lamb called Shepherd's Pie.

1 large onion, chopped

2 pounds steak, minced

2 tablespoons tomato paste

1½ cups water or red wine

chopped carrots (optional)

4 large russet potatoes, about 3¼ pounds

4 to 6 tablespoons butter

white pepper to taste

½ cup whole milk

Sauté onions, steak, tomato paste, water and carrots for approximately 10 minutes. Boil and drain potatoes, transferring to a bowl. Mash potatoes with butter and white pepper. Add a little milk and whip potatoes with a fork. Pour steak mixture into 9-inch pie dish. Spread potatoes on top. Cook at 355 degrees 45 minutes. Broil until potatoes are browned.

Yield: 6 to 8 servings

October 20, 2001, JLE-NS presented Lady Thatcher on the campus of Northwestern University. Lady Thatcher was honored at Patron Reception and spoke to an audience of over 1,000 on Challenges Facing the 21st Century and The War on Terrorism.

Dark Ale Beef

Served with a nice red wine, this makes for a perfect winter supper.

2 tablespoons olive oil

6 slices bacon, cut into ½-inch strips

2½ pound rump roast, cut into 6 equal pieces

1 tablespoon kosher salt

½ teaspoon pepper

¼ teaspoon ground allspice

1 pound onions, peeled and sliced

2 garlic cloves, crushed

2 cups canned tomatoes

2 (12-ounce) bottles dark beer

2 tablespoons light brown sugar

1 tablespoon minced thyme

1 tablespoon minced rosemary

8 Yukon Gold or Yellow Finn potatoes, peeled and cut into 1½-inch chunks

Place oil and bacon in a large ovenproof stockpot. Cook bacon until crispy. Remove bacon and set aside. Season beef with salt, pepper and allspice. Sear in drippings 3 to 4 minutes per side until browned. Remove beef. Brown onions and garlic in pot. Return bacon and beef. Add tomatoes, beer, brown sugar, thyme and rosemary. Bring to simmer. Cover pot and place on bottom rack of 350 degree oven. Simmer 10 minutes. If not simmering, increase heat to 375 degrees. Cook about 2 hours or until meat is tender. Add potatoes and cook another 30 minutes until potatoes are tender. Serve hot.

Yield: 6 servings

New York Steak, New York Strip, Delmonico Steak, Kansas City Steak, Kansas City Strip, shell steak, sirloin club steak, strip steak. It's all the same steak. Its name depends on where you live.

Flank Steak Marinade

Tired of chicken and burgers on the grill?
This turns grilling into a gourmet experience.

¼ cup Madeira or white
or red wine

2 tablespoons olive oil

1 tablespoon minced garlic

1 teaspoon kosher salt

1 teaspoon pepper

½ teaspoon dried rosemary

½ teaspoon ground thyme

½ teaspoon ground marjoram

1 tablespoon minced shallots or
sliced green onions

1 (2 to 3-pound) flank steak

Combine wine, oil, garlic, salt, pepper, rosemary, thyme,
marjoram and shallots in a large zip-top plastic bag. Mix well. Add meat
and turn to coat. Refrigerate at least 1 hour or up to 24 hours.
Grill or broil to desired degree of doneness.

Yield: 4 servings

Have leftover wine? Pour it into an ice tray and freeze.
Next day, throw the cubes into a baggie and keep in freezer.
When a recipe calls for wine, use the cubes
instead of opening a bottle of wine.

Old World Brisket

Tangy and spicy, we love this one.

¼ cup coarsely ground pepper
1 (4-pound) boneless beef brisket
⅔ cup soy sauce
1 garlic clove, minced

½ cup vinegar
1 tablespoon tomato sauce
1 teaspoon paprika

Press pepper into meat coating entire surface. Place brisket in a
13 x 9 x 2-inch baking dish. Combine soy sauce, garlic, vinegar, tomato
sauce and paprika. Carefully spoon marinade over meat. Avoid loosening
the pepper. Cover and refrigerate overnight, turning once. Remove from
marinade. Wrap tightly in heavy-duty foil. Place in a roasting pan and
bake at 300 degrees 4 hours. Thinly slice meat and serve hot or cold.

Yield: 8 servings

Rumor has it that there are more
hot dog joints in the Chicago area than McDonalds,
Wendy's, and Burger Kings combined.

Mexican Lasagna

Here is a twist to the usual lasagna.

1 pound ground beef
½ onion, chopped
1 (15-ounce) can chili beans
1 (8-ounce) can tomato sauce
1 (4-ounce) can chopped
green chilies

1 (1¼-ounce) package
taco seasoning
6 flour tortillas, halved
1 (8-ounce) package shredded
Cheddar cheese
avocado and sour cream
for garnish

Brown beef and onions. Add beans, tomato sauce, chilies
and seasoning. Mix well. Layer half the tortillas in the bottom of an
8 x 8 x 2 or 9 x 9 x 2-inch baking dish. Spread half the meat mixture and
sprinkle with half the cheese. Repeat layers. Bake at 350 degrees 30 minutes.
Cool 10 minutes before serving. Serve with avocado and sour cream.

Yield: 4 to 6 servings

150

Almond Crusted Halibut with Cipollini Onions and Mascarpone Spinach

Contributed by Chef Victor Hernandez
of The Stained Glass Restaurant, Evanston.

1 cup panko bread crumbs
½ cup sliced almonds
1 stick butter, melted
¼ cup grated Parmesan cheese
2 tablespoons chopped parsley
1 garlic clove, minced

4 (5 to 6-ounce) halibut fillets
salt and pepper to taste
1 cup mascarpone cheese
1 pound spinach, shredded
½ pound cipollini onions
  or pearl onions
butter

Combine bread crumbs, almonds, butter, Parmesan cheese, parsley and garlic. Place fillets on a buttered nonstick baking sheet. Season with salt and pepper. Cover each fillet with ¼ -inch layer of the bread crumb mixture. Bake at 425 degrees 12 to 15 minutes or until fillet flakes easily and the crust is golden brown. Melt mascarpone cheese in a saucepan over low heat. Add spinach and increase heat to medium. Cook until spinach is wilted and bright green, stirring constantly. Season with salt and pepper. Sauté onions in butter at medium heat until tender and golden brown. To serve, place a spoonful of spinach in the center of a dinner plate. Spoon onions around spinach. Place halibut on top of spinach and serve immediately.

Yield: 4 servings

Turbot and Shrimp with Candy Cane Beets, Choy Sum Fennel and a Candied Lemon Essence

Contributed by Chef Mark Grosz of Oceanique, Evanston.

1 lemon, seeded and finely diced

1 cup sugar

2 cups water

1 tablespoon olive oil

12 baby candy cane beets

1 tablespoon extra virgin olive oil

salt and pepper to taste

1 teaspoon 6 to 8 year old balsamic vinegar

1 bulb fennel, peeled and cut into ¼ -inch slices

2 tablespoons grapeseed oil

1 tablespoon extra virgin olive oil

½ cup Sauvignon Blanc

1 teaspoon shallot, minced

2 tablespoons unsalted butter, room temperature

2 cups choy sum or other Chinese green

1 garlic clove, minced

2 tablespoons extra virgin olive oil

16 shrimp, medium size

2 tablespoons extra virgin olive oil

16 ounces turbot fillets

2 tablespoons unsalted butter, softened

Sea salt and freshly ground black pepper to taste

To make candied lemon, boil lemon with sugar and water 20 minutes or until tender. Strain lemon and set aside. Rub beets with oil. Roast beets at 350 degrees about 20 to 25 minutes or until a knife slides through easily. Peel and slice in half. Season with salt, pepper, oil and vinegar. Keep warm. Blanch fennel in boiling water for 3 minutes and dry. Sauté in grapeseed oil until lightly browned on both sides. Season with salt, pepper and oil. Cook and stir wine and shallot until reduced to 2 tablespoons. Whisk in butter and 1 tablespoon candied lemon on low heat. Season with salt and pepper.

Keep sauce warm. Sauté choy sum and garlic in oil. Season with salt and pepper. Keep warm. Sauté shrimp in oil and reserve. Season turbot with salt and pepper. Sauté in butter 2 to 3 minutes per side or until lightly browned on both sides. To serve, spoon half of choy sum and half of fennel on each plate. Place fillet on top. Scatter half the beets around the plate. Fold shrimp into wine sauce (do not boil) and spoon over fish. Top with remaining choy sum and fennel.

Yield: 4 servings

Chef's Wine Recommendation: A creamy White Bordeaux would enhance the shrimp-turbot combination quite nicely, such as Château Fieuzal Blanc.

Parmesan Tilapia

Contributed by Burhop's Seafood, Wilmette.

¼ cup grated Parmesan cheese

¼ cup bread crumbs

2 tablespoons dried parsley

1 teaspoon garlic powder

1 tablespoon olive oil

1 tablespoon lemon juice

4 tilapia fillets

Combine cheese, bread crumbs, parsley and garlic powder. Set aside. Heat a large skillet. Add oil and juice. Sauté fillets 3 minutes per side. Sprinkle cheese mixture on fillets. Sauté each side for 1 minute. Serve immediately.

Yield: 4 servings

Orange-Horseradish Crusted Salmon with Lentils de Puy

Contributed by Chef Jeffrey Tomchek, Deer Path Inn, Lake Forest.

- ORANGE-HORSERADISH CRUST -

Zest from 1 orange, avoid the white pith because it will make the crust bitter

Juice from 1 orange

1½ tablespoons prepared horseradish

½ cup bread crumbs

½ cup unsalted butter, softened

1 bunch dill, minced

Combine zest, juice, horseradish, bread crumbs, butter and dill in a mixer with the paddle attachment. Beat until completely mixed. Refrigerate until chilled completely. The crust can be made several days ahead if desired.

- FRENCH STYLE LENTILS -

1 pound Lentils de Puy, these dark green, tiny lentils can be found at specialty food shops

3 tablespoons diced carrot

3 tablespoons diced yellow onions

Sea salt and ground pepper to taste

Rinse lentils thoroughly under cold water. Combine lentils, carrots and onions in a saucepan. Add enough water to just cover. Cook over medium heat until the lentils are al dente. If they absorb all the water before they are cooked, add more water. If there is water left after they are cooked, drain the excess and discard. Season with the salt and pepper. May refrigerate and save for several days or use immediately.

- VINAIGRETTE -

2 tablespoons Dijon mustard

¼ cup balsamic vinegar

¾ cup good quality olive oil

Sea salt and freshly
ground pepper to taste

Combine mustard and vinegar in a mixing bowl. Slowly whisk in oil until creamy. Season with salt and pepper. If you do not like the flavor of olive oil in a dressing you can substitute canola oil.

- SALMON -

2½ pounds fresh salmon fillet, skin and pin bones removed

Roll chilled crust mixture out between two sheets of plastic wrap to the size and shape of the salmon fillets. Season salmon with salt and pepper. Cover the salmon with crust and trim excess so salmon is neatly covered. Roast at 450 degrees to desired degree of doneness. I think salmon is best cooked just a little past medium. When salmon is almost done, heat lentils in a saucepan with a little vinaigrette. Divide the lentils on four plates. Top each with one-fourth of salmon. Drizzle remaining vinaigrette over salmon and serve.

Yield: 4 servings

Salmon is a rare fish that pairs well with some red wines. Jeff likes this dish with a Pinot Noir from Oregon State.

Red Snapper with Mango Relish

Contributed by Metropolitan Café, Highland Park.

- MANGO RELISH -

1 mango, diced
½ pineapple, diced
½ red bell pepper, diced

2 tablespoons finely
chopped cilantro
1 tablespoon lemon juice
salt and pepper to taste

Combine mango, pineapple, peppers, cilantro, juice, salt and pepper.

- SIMPLE RISOTTO -

½ cup chopped red onions
½ cup diced celery
1 cup risotto
4 cups chicken stock

½ cup butter
½ cup white wine
salt and pepper to taste

Sauté onions, celery and risotto for 10 minutes. Slowly add 1 cup chicken stock at a time and cook until absorbed. Add butter and wine allowing risotto to absorb the liquid before adding more. Takes 15 minutes. Season with salt and pepper. Cook until risotto is al dente. Serve immediately.

- SNAPPER -

12 ounces red snapper   Greek salad dressing

Marinate snapper in dressing. Bake at 350 degrees 10 minutes.
Spoon mango relish over snapper. Serve with risotto.

Yield: 4 servings

Marlin, Tuna or Swordfish Steak Marinade

Fantastic!

2 fish steaks, rinsed

1/4 cup chopped onions

1/2 cup diced Roma tomatoes

2 tablespoons olive oil

1 tablespoon lemon juice

1/2 teaspoon ground cumin

1/2 teaspoon dried mustard

1 tablespoon dried cilantro

1 teaspoon Tabasco sauce (optional)

Place fish on greased foil. Combine onions, tomatoes, oil, lemon juice, cumin, mustard, cilantro and Tabasco. Mix well. Pour mixture over fish. Wrap foil to form a pouch. Grill to desired degree of doneness. For well done, grill 20 to 25 minutes depending on thickness of fish.

Yield: 2 servings

Low Country Boil

A classic.

1/4 cup Old Bay seasoning or 1 pouch shrimp spice or crab boil

2 pounds kielbasa turkey sausage, cut into 2-inch pieces

6 ears corn-on-the-cob, shucked and cleaned

2 pounds shrimp with shell on, rinsed

Melted butter and cocktail sauce

Fill a large stockpot with water and add Old Bay seasoning. Bring to boil. Add sausage and boil 5 minutes. Add corn and boil 7 to 10 minutes. Add shrimp and boil 3 to 5 minutes or until pink. Drain and place in a large bowl. Spread on newspapers covering your table. Everyone peels and enjoys their own shrimp. Provide butter and cocktail sauce.

Yield: 6 servings

Ropa Vieja-Braised Beef, Peppers and Onions

Contributed by Corner Cooks, Winnetka.

3 pounds skirt or flank steak, trimmed

2 quarts water

2 carrots, coarsely chopped

1 large onion, coarsely chopped

2 stalks celery, coarsely chopped

1 bay leaf

3 garlic cloves, crushed lightly

1 teaspoon dried oregano

1 teaspoon ground cumin

1 teaspoon salt

1/4 teaspoon whole black peppercorns

2 bell peppers, cut into 1/4-inch strips

1 red onion, cut into 1/4-inch strips

2 tablespoons olive oil

1 (14 to 16-ounce) can whole tomatoes with juice, chopped

3 tablespoons tomato paste

3 garlic cloves, minced

1 teaspoon ground cumin

1/4 teaspoon dried oregano

salt and pepper to taste

2 red bell peppers, cut into 1/4-inch strips

2 yellow bell peppers, cut into 1/4-inch strips

2 tablespoons olive oil

1 cup frozen peas, thawed

1/2 cup pimiento-stuffed Spanish olives, drained and halved

Combine steak, water, carrots, onions, celery, bay leaf, garlic, oregano, cumin, salt and peppercorns in a 5-quart stockpot. Simmer 1 hour, 30 minutes or until beef is tender. Remove from heat. Cool meat in stock for 30 minutes. Transfer meat to a platter and cover. Strain the braising stock into a bowl. Return stock to stockpot. Boil 30 minutes until reduced to 3 cups. Save stock. Stew may be made up to this point 1 day ahead. Refrigerate beef and braising stock separately. In a 5-quart stockpot, sauté peppers and onions in oil over moderate heat, stirring, until softened. Shred meat into 3 x 1/2-inch pieces. Add shredded meat, 2 cups braising stock, tomatoes with juice, tomato paste, garlic, cumin, oregano, salt and pepper. Simmer 20 minutes. In a large skillet, sauté sweet red and yellow peppers in oil over moderate heat, stirring occasionally, until softened. Stir into stew. Add enough additional braising stock to thin to desired consistency. Simmer 5 minutes. Stir in peas and olives. Simmer 5 minutes more.

Yield: 8 to 10 servings

Mussels

This is such an easy inexpensive dish to make.
Serve with a crusty bread to soak up the remaining juice. Discard any mussels that are open prior to being cooked and any mussels that do not open after being cooked.

2 tablespoons minced garlic
1 tablespoon olive oil
2 tablespoons chopped oregano
2 tablespoons chopped parsley
1 (16-ounce) can tomatoes

1 (12-ounce) jar clam juice
1 cup white wine
salt and pepper to taste
1 pound mussels

Cook garlic in oil until tender in a large stockpot.
Purée oregano, parsley, tomatoes, clam juice, wine, salt and pepper in a food processor until smooth. Add mixture to garlic. Bring to boil and add mussels. Cook until the shells open and meat easily pulls from the shell. If they do not, continue cooking until they do.

Yield: 4 servings

Island Red Snapper

This recipe closely resembles a traditional
Caribbean dish and it is very easy to make. Garnish with lime wedges.
Serve with warm tortillas and a rum drink and you are all set.

1 tablespoon olive oil

½ onion, chopped

1 (4-ounce) can diced
mild green chilies

5 tablespoons chopped cilantro

3 garlic gloves, chopped

1 (14-ounce) can stewed tomatoes

salt and pepper to taste

1 to 1½ pounds red snapper fillets

lime wedges for garnish

warm tortillas

Heat oil in large skillet. Sauté onions 2 to 3 minutes. Add green chilies,
half the cilantro and garlic. Sauté about 2 to 3 minutes. Add tomatoes with
juice, breaking up the tomatoes while they cook. Season fish with salt and
pepper and place on top of sauce. Bring to simmer. Cover and reduce
heat to medium-low. Simmer 8 to 10 minutes until fish is opaque in center.
Transfer fish to a platter. Continue to simmer sauce until thickened, if
needed. Spoon sauce over fish. Garnish with remaining
cilantro and lime wedges. Serve with warm tortillas.

Yield: 4 servings

Sesame Encrusted Ahi Tuna

The key to this dish is finding a fresh high quality piece of tuna.

3 garlic cloves, minced

3 tablespoons chopped ginger

3 tablespoons chopped green onions

1½ tablespoons chopped cilantro

¾ cup sherry

¾ cup oyster sauce

¾ cup low sodium soy sauce

3 tablespoons sesame oil

3 tablespoons olive oil

1½ teaspoons cornstarch, mixed with small amount of water

3 pinches crushed red pepper to taste

3 teaspoons sugar to taste

4 (8-ounce) ahi tuna fillets

¼ cup sesame seeds, toasted

wasabi for garnish

Combine garlic, ginger, green onions and cilantro. Set aside. In a saucepan, whisk together sherry, oyster sauce, soy sauce, sesame oil and olive oil. Bring to boil. Whisk in cornstarch mixture and reduce to low heat. Stir until thickened. Add garlic mixture and simmer 2 to 3 minutes. Remove from heat and add red pepper and sugar. Place tuna in a zip-top plastic bag. Pour in marinade to cover fillets, reserving remaining marinade. Marinate 30 minutes. Roll tuna in sesame seeds. Grill or pan fry tuna 2 to 3 minutes per side. Tuna will be medium rare. Pour remaining marinade over tuna and serve with wasabi.

Yield: 4 servings

Sweet Baby Ray's BBQ Baby Back Ribs

Contributed by Sweet Baby Ray's.

4 slabs babyback ribs, skinned

salt, pepper and onion salt to taste

8 ounces apple, cherry or hickory chips, soaked in water

1 (16-ounce) bottle Sweet Baby Ray's BBQ Sauce

Place 52 coals in center of grill and burn for 30 minutes. Arrange 26 coals on each side and put greased pan in middle of grill basin. Generously sprinkle both sides of ribs with salt, pepper and onion salt. Stand ribs on rib rack in center of grill. Cook 30 minutes and then rotate ribs, inside to outside and from top to bottom. Add soaked wood chips and six charcoal briquettes to each side of coals. After 30 minutes, rotate ribs again. Check ribs every 15 minutes and rotate when necessary. Ribs are cooked after 2 hours or when easily pierced with a fork. Remove them from rack and place the ribs upside down in center of grill. Generously brush barbecue sauce on ribs and place ribs side by side, 2 high, in center of grill. Cover and cook for 10 minutes. Turn ribs over, apply sauce to top of ribs and cook another 10 minutes. Serve and enjoy!

Yield: 4 to 6 servings

Herb-Crusted Pork with New Potatoes

2 pounds new potatoes
¼ cup butter, melted
2 tablespoons horseradish
½ teaspoon salt
½ teaspoon pepper
½ cup fine dry bread crumbs
½ cup Parmesan cheese
½ cup chopped fresh basil

3 tablespoons olive oil
1 tablespoon pepper
1 teaspoon kosher salt
3 tablespoons chopped
  fresh thyme
1½ pounds pork tenderloins
2 tablespoons chopped
  fresh parsley

Peel a 1-inch strip around the center of each potato, leaving skin on ends. Place potatoes in a large bowl. Add butter, horseradish, salt and pepper, tossing gently. Arrange potatoes on a lightly greased rack on a broiler pan. Bake at 425 degrees 20 minutes. Remove from oven. Combine bread crumbs, cheese, basil, oil, pepper and salt. Moisten pork with water. Press bread crumb mixture into tenderloin. Place on rack with potatoes. Bake at 425 degrees 25 minutes or until a meat thermometer inserted into pork reaches 160 degrees and potatoes are tender. Sprinkle potatoes with parsley and slice tenderloin.

Yield: 4 servings

Pork Tenderloin with Apples and Onions

This is on the sweeter side and fantastic served with savory vegetables.

1 large onion, chopped

3 Granny Smith apples, peeled and sliced

olive oil

1 (2-pound) pork tenderloin

⅓ cup butter

1 cup orange juice

½ cup packed brown sugar

1 teaspoon cinnamon

½ teaspoon ground ginger

⅛ teaspoon ground cloves

cooked white or wild rice

Sauté onions and apples in oil. Transfer to a bowl. Add pork and brown over high heat. Bake at 375 degrees 45 minutes. Combine butter, juice, brown sugar, cinnamon, ginger and cloves in a saucepan. Simmer 5 minutes. Add apples and onions. Heat thoroughly. Serve pork over rice with sauce.

Yield: 4 to 6 servings

164

Oriental Babyback Ribs

Everyone needs a great barbecue rib recipe. Give this one a try.

- BARBECUE SAUCE -

1 medium Vidalia onion, chopped	2 cups ketchup
4 tablespoons butter	¼ cup rice vinegar
1 tablespoon minced garlic	2 tablespoons soy sauce
½ cup packed brown sugar	2 tablespoons Worcestershire sauce
¼ cup grated ginger	1 tablespoon liquid smoke

Sauté onions in butter 5 minutes until tender. Cool slightly. Pulse onions in a food processor until coarsely puréed. Add garlic and pulse. Add brown sugar, ginger, ketchup, vinegar, soy sauce, Worcestershire sauce and liquid smoke, one at a time, to processor and pulse briefly after each addition.

- MARINADE -

½ cup olive oil	1 tablespoon dried thyme
⅓ cup red wine or	1 teaspoon dry mustard or
12 ounces flat beer	2 teaspoons prepared mustard
2 tablespoons soy sauce	2 slabs babyback ribs
1 tablespoon rice vinegar	

Whisk together oil, red wine, soy sauce, vinegar, thyme and mustard. Pour over ribs. Refrigerate at least 8 hours or overnight, turning occasionally. Place ribs in a dark enameled roasting pan with an elevated rack. Cover and bake at 450 degrees 15 minutes. Reduce heat to 350 degrees and bake 30 minutes more. Prepare a charcoal fire and allow to burn down to glowing coals with white ash. Cook ribs over coals 20 to 30 minutes, turning every few minutes. Baste with barbecue sauce the last few minutes. Serve with remaining sauce.

Yield: 4 servings

Rosemary Pork Tenderloin

Rosemary is a wonderful herb. This is easy and perfect for a week night dinner.

2 teaspoons pepper	2 teaspoons olive oil
1 teaspoon dried rosemary	1 (14-ounce) can beef stock
¾ teaspoon salt	¼ cup dry sherry
1 garlic clove, minced	1 tablespoon tomato paste
1 teaspoon olive oil	6 (2-ounce) French bread rolls
1 (1-pound) pork tenderloin	

Combine pepper, rosemary, salt, garlic and oil. Rub over pork. Heat 2 teaspoons oil in a large oven-proof skillet over medium-high heat. Brown pork 4 minutes on all sides. Bake at 400 degrees 10 minutes. Thinly slice pork and keep warm. Return skillet to stove top. Add stock and scrape to loosen browned bits. Whisk in sherry and tomato paste. Bring to boil. Reduce heat and simmer 5 minutes. Serve pork on rolls with sauce.

Yield: 6 servings

Vegetarian Jambalaya

Contributed by Charles Murray of Cajun Charlie's Grill in Evanston and
dedicated to his mother, Mrs. Barbara J. Murray.

1½ tablespoons butter

3 onions, chopped

2 green bell peppers, chopped

2 cups finely chopped green onions

4 plum tomatoes, finely chopped

3 garlic cloves, minced

1 cup sliced zucchini

1 tablespoon dried oregano

1 teaspoon minced thyme

⅛ teaspoon chili powder

⅛ teaspoon cayenne pepper

1¼ cups white rice uncooked or
brown rice, parboiled

1¼ cups tomato purée

4 cups unsalted chicken stock

1 teaspoon salt

1 cup chopped red bell peppers,
1-inch pieces

1 cup sliced portabello mushrooms

½ teaspoon coarse black pepper

Melt the butter over medium heat. Sauté onions, green peppers,
green onions and plum tomatoes 10 minutes, stirring frequently. Add garlic,
zucchini, oregano, thyme, chili powder and cayenne. Sauté
2 more minutes. Mix in rice, tomato purée, stock and salt. Bring to boil.
Stir until tomato purée is mixed in. Cover, reduce heat and simmer
25 minutes. Add red peppers and mushrooms. Cook another
5 minutes until peppers, mushrooms and rice are cooked.
Season with pepper and serve immediately.

Yield: 5 servings

Chicken Tikka

Contributed by Rizvana Adanjee, Junior League of Evanston-North Shore scholarship recipient.

A delicious fragrant chicken. Serve with basmati rice, naan or any other Indian-inspired side dish.

2 tablespoons fresh lime juice

1 teaspoon chopped ginger

1 garlic clove, crushed

1 teaspoon chili powder

1 teaspoon red Kashmiri chili powder

1 teaspoon pepper

2 tablespoons vegetable oil

1½ teaspoons salt

2¼ pounds chicken breast, cut into large cubes

Combine juice, ginger, garlic, chili powder, red chili powder, pepper, oil and salt in a bowl. Cut slits in chicken. Add chicken pieces and toss to coat. Cover and refrigerate at least 6 hours. Thread the chicken pieces onto skewers and grill over hot charcoal for 10 to 15 minutes.

Yield: 6 servings

Arroz con Pollo

6 boneless skinless chicken breast halves

1 large onion, finely chopped

1 large green bell pepper, finely chopped

3 garlic cloves, mashed

1/2 (15-ounce) can tomato sauce

1 bay leaf

1 teaspoon Bijol

2 tablespoons chopped cilantro

2 tablespoons capers

10 olives, chopped

1 (12-ounce) can beer

2 cups water

1 1/4 cups dry rice

peas and pimentos for garnish

Brown chicken in an oven safe pot. Add onions, peppers and garlic. Cook 15 minutes. Add tomato sauce, bay leaf, bijol, cilantro, capers and olives. Simmer 5 minutes. Add beer and water. Stir in rice. Bring to boil. Cover pot and place in a 350 degree oven. Bake 20 minutes, stirring occasionally. Add more beer if rice is too dry. Cook an additional 10 minutes until rice is done and has absorbed all liquid. Arrange peas and pimentos on top. Let stand 5 minutes before serving.

Yield: 8 servings

Chicken Enchiladas

A great recipe for a Mexican favorite.

1 medium onion, diced
4 tablespoons butter
2½ cups chicken stock
¼ cup all-purpose flour
1 (8-ounce) container sour cream
3 cups cooked and diced chicken
½ teaspoon chili powder

1½ cups shredded Cheddar cheese
1 (4-ounce) can diced green chilies (optional)
1 (2-ounce) jar diced pimentos or 1 sweet red pepper, chopped
10 to 12 soft flour tortillas
½ cup shredded Cheddar cheese

Sauté onions in butter until tender. Add stock and bring to boil. Whisk in flour. Stir until mixture thickens. Stir in sour cream. Remove from heat and cool. Combine chicken, chili powder, cheese, chilies and pimentos and 1 cup onion mixture. Dip tortillas in remaining onion mixture. Evenly divide chicken mixture and place in center of each tortilla. Roll up and place on a large greased baking sheet. Top with cheese. Bake at 350 degrees 30 minutes or until cheese melts.

Yield: 6 to 8 servings

Chicken Marbella

4 boneless, skinless chicken breasts halves

1 head garlic, cloves peeled

¼ cup dried oregano

coarse salt and pepper

½ cup red wine vinegar

½ cup olive oil

1 cup pitted prunes

½ cup pitted Spanish olives

½ cup capers with juice

6 bay leaves

1 cup packed brown sugar

1 cup white wine

¼ cup chopped cilantro

Combine chicken, garlic, oregano, salt, pepper, vinegar, oil, prunes, olives, capers and bay leaves in a 13 x 9 x 2-inch baking dish. Cover and refrigerate overnight. Top with brown sugar, wine and cilantro. Bake, uncovered, at 350 degrees 50 minutes to 1 hour.

Yield: 4 servings

Thai Chicken

Easy and delicious. Add vegetables such as zucchini,
onions and portobello mushrooms for a hearty meal.

4 boneless, skinless chicken
breast halves

2 to 3 garlic cloves, minced

4 teaspoons minced fresh ginger

¼ teaspoon crushed red pepper

¼ cup packed brown sugar

¼ cup distilled white vinegar

3 tablespoons soy sauce

1 teaspoon fish sauce or oyster
sauce to taste

4 green onions, thinly sliced

Sauté chicken until done. Remove chicken and keep warm. Add garlic to
drippings in skillet. Sauté until firm. Add ginger, red pepper, brown sugar,
vinegar, soy sauce and fish sauce. Cook and stir until slightly thickened.
Pour sauce over warm chicken. Top with onions and serve.

Yield: 4 servings

Garlic Chicken

If you love garlic, this is the recipe for you!

½ cup Parmesan cheese

2 tablespoons minced parsley

1 teaspoon dried oregano

4 garlic cloves, minced

¼ cup dry bread crumbs

¼ teaspoon pepper

2 boneless, skinless chicken
breasts halves

3 tablespoons butter, melted

Combine cheese, parsley, oregano, garlic, bread crumbs and pepper.
Dip chicken in butter and dredge in cheese mixture. Place in an
8 x 8 x 2-inch baking dish. Drizzle remaining butter over chicken.
Bake at 375 degrees 30 minutes.

Yield: 2 servings

Green Curry Chicken

Why go out for Thai food when you can make it at home?
May substitute 1½ pounds shrimp for chicken and fish stock for chicken stock.
Add shrimp just before adding basil. You can easily make fish stock by boiling
shrimp shells in 1½ cups water. Boil until reduced to 1 cup.

2 tablespoons vegetable oil
2 cups diced eggplant
½ cup chopped onions
1 cup thinly sliced red bell peppers
2 teaspoons minced garlic
2 to 4 tablespoons Thai green curry paste
1 tablespoon finely grated lime zest
2 tablespoons Thai fish sauce

1 pound boneless, skinless chicken breast halves, cut into strips
1 (14-ounce) can unsweetened coconut milk
1 cup chicken stock
½ cup chopped basil
¼ teaspoon salt
steamed white rice
lime slices for garnish

Heat oil in a wok or large sauté pan. Sauté eggplant, onions
and peppers 3 to 5 minutes until tender. Add garlic and cook 2 minutes.
Stir in curry paste, zest and fish sauce. Cook and stir 15 minutes. Add
chicken, coconut milk and stock. Bring to boil. Reduce heat and simmer
until thickened. Stir in basil and salt. Remove from heat.
Serve over rice. Garnish with lime slices.

Yield: 4 to 6 servings

Want to prevent clumped rice?
A few drops of lemon juice added to simmering
rice will keep the grains separate.

Chicken with Peanut Sauce

Peanut sauce is not difficult to make,
but your guests will think you spent hours on it.

- CHICKEN -

6 boneless, skinless chicken breast
halves, cut into strips
1 tablespoon vegetable oil
1 tablespoon soy sauce

1 tablespoon honey
1 tablespoon minced garlic
1 tablespoon ground ginger
1 tablespoon curry powder

Combine chicken, oil, soy sauce, honey, garlic, ginger and curry in a bowl.
Mix to coat. Thread chicken onto skewers. Grill 10 minutes.

- HOT PEANUT SAUCE -

1 cup chicken stock
2 tablespoons soy sauce
2 tablespoons vinegar

1 teaspoon sesame or olive oil
5 tablespoons creamy
peanut butter

Blend stock, soy sauce, vinegar and oil in a saucepan. Bring to simmer.
Stir in peanut butter until smooth. Serve with chicken strips.

Yield: 6 servings

Grilled Chicken Breast
with Apple Mayonnaise

Poultry and apples compliment each other wonderfully.

1 cup mayonnaise

1½ cups cider or apple juice

salt and white pepper to taste

4 boneless, skinless chicken breast halves

1 Granny Smith apple, peeled, cored and cut into small cubes

Blend mayonnaise and enough cider to make mixture a pouring consistency. Add pepper. Sprinkle chicken with salt and pepper. Grill to desired degree of doneness. Slice chicken. To serve, place chicken slices on a plate. Sprinkle apple pieces on top and pour apple mayonnaise to personal liking.

Yield: 4 servings

Chicken with Mozzarella and Sun-Dried Tomatoes

You can use provolone cheese instead of the mozzarella, if you please.

4 boneless, skinless chicken breast halves

4 ounces mozzarella cheese, cut into 4 thick slices

1 (8-ounce) jar sun-dried tomatoes in oil, drained

pepper to taste

2 tablespoons olive oil

8 thin slices Parma ham

chopped basil for garnish

Cut a long horizontal slit through the thickest part of each chicken breast without cutting through. Stuff a cheese slice and tomatoes into pocket. Sprinkle with pepper. Heat oil in a skillet. Brown chicken 4 minutes per side. Transfer to a baking dish. Bake at 400 degrees 15 minutes. Cook ham in the skillet 1 minute or until crispy. Place ham on individual plates. Place chicken on ham and garnish with basil.

Yield: 4 servings

Picnic Lemon Turkey

1½ cups lemon juice

1¼ cups vegetable oil

4 garlic cloves, minced

4 teaspoons pepper

2 tablespoons dried dill

3 tablespoons teriyaki sauce

½ cup chopped onion

2 (6 to 7-pound) turkey breasts
or 1 (12 to 15-pound) turkey

Blend juice, oil, garlic, pepper, dill, teriyaki sauce and onions. Place turkey in a large pan or plastic bag. Pour lemon marinade over turkey. Refrigerate 8 to 12 hours or overnight, basting with marinade. Remove from marinade. Roast at 325 degrees 3 hours, 30 minutes to 4 hours, 30 minutes. Baste with marinade while roasting. Refrigerate and wrap for a picnic entrée.

Yield: 8 to 10 servings

Desserts

Highland Park History

The land upon which the present city of Highland Park was secured by the U.S. government from the Potawatomi Indians in 1833, after which the land was open to settlement. At this point, the Green Bay Road blazed a trail from Chicago to Green Bay, serving as a mail route and lined with log cabins and inns for the travelers.

Officially incorporated in 1869, the name of Highland Park was given to the city in 1854 by Walter Gurnee, President of the Chicago and Northwestern Railroad Company. During the Civil War, he bought all the land in the area and sold it for $32.00 per acre. This started the "building boom" when many wealthy Chicagoans invested in this area.

Highland Park continued to thrive, particularly after the Chicago and Milwaukee Electric Railway Company opened Ravinia Park as a year-round amusement park. When the Railway Company failed, the park was taken over by the Ravinia Company and began to offer musical programs. Under the leadership of Louis Eckstein, Ravinia festival was born. Summer home to the Chicago Symphony Orchestra, the festival today is known internationally as an outdoor venue for both classical and contemporary music.

Highland Park's unique blend of city dining and entertainment with a suburban lifestyle and the mix of upscale shops in the renovated downtown continue to attract people from all over the Chicago area.

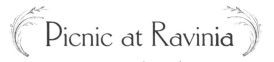 Picnic at Ravinia

Ravinia is a unique outdoor theater experience.
With a sunken amphitheater, a flat grassy area with tall trees,
this is a place where you can watch the stars (above or on stage)
and hear some of the greatest music in the world. Finely
appointed picnic baskets, including candles, abound!

Shrimp Dip

Goat Cheese Tarts

Picnic Lemon Turkey

Tarragon Green Beans

Summer Coleslaw

Blue Cheese Potato Salad

Lemon Meltaways

Angel Cookies

Pecan Pie

Contributed by Mayor Michael D. Belsky, Highland Park.

1 cup light corn syrup	1 teaspoon vanilla
1 cup packed dark brown sugar	3 large eggs, slightly beaten
¼ teaspoon salt	1 heaping cup pecan halves
⅓ cup butter, melted	1 (9-inch) pie shell, unbaked

Combine corn syrup, brown sugar, salt, butter and vanilla. Mix well.
Add eggs and blend well. Stir in pecans. Pour filling into pie shell.
Bake at 350 degrees 45 minutes or until set.

Yield: 8 servings

When measuring honey or syrup,
coat the cup or spoon with vegetable oil spray.
The honey or syrup will slide out easily.

Chocolate-Kahlúa Cheesecake

Contributed by Chief Shafer, Highland Park Police Department.

- CHOCOLATE CRUMB CRUST -

1⅓ cups chocolate wafer cookie crumbs

1 tablespoon sugar

¼ cup unsalted butter, softened

Combine cookie crumbs, sugar and butter. Mix well.
Press mixture into the bottom of a 9-inch springform pan.

- CHEESECAKE -

1½ cups semi-sweet chocolate chips

⅛ cup butter

¼ cup Kahlúa

2 (8-ounce) package cream cheese, softened and cut into pieces

2 large eggs

⅓ cup sugar

¼ teaspoon salt

1 cup sour cream

- MOCHA SAUCE -

1 (6-ounce) package semi-sweet chocolate chips

⅓ cup Kahlúa

⅓ cup light corn syrup

CHEESECAKE DIRECTIONS: Heat chocolate chips, butter and Kahlúa in a small saucepan. Stir until chocolate melts and is smooth. Cool slightly. Beat cream cheese until smooth. Beat in eggs. Add sugar, salt and sour cream and beat until smooth. Gradually stir in chocolate mixture. Pour mixture into crust. Bake at 325 degrees 40 minutes or until barely set in the center. Remove from oven. Cool at room temperature at least 1 hour. To serve, spread a thin layer of sour cream on top of cake. Drizzle with mocha sauce. Store refrigerated.

MOCHA SAUCE DIRECTIONS: Combine chocolate chips, Kahlúa and corn syrup in a saucepan. Cook and stir until chocolate melts and is smooth.

Yield: 12 to 15 servings

The Original Barbara Bush Chocolate Chip Cookie Recipe

Contributed by Former First Lady, Barbara Bush.

1 cup butter, softened

1 cup sugar

1 cup packed brown sugar

2 eggs

2 cups all-purpose flour

1 teaspoon baking soda

1 teaspoon salt

2 cups quick-cooking rolled oats

2 teaspoons vanilla

1 (12-ounce) package semi-sweet chocolate chips

Cream butter, sugar and brown sugar. Add eggs and beat until smooth. Sift together flour, baking soda and salt. Add to creamed mixture. Stir in oats, vanilla and chocolate chips. Drop dough by tablespoonfuls onto an ungreased baking sheet. Bake at 350 degrees 10 minutes.

Yield: 4 dozen

In 1999, JLE-NS celebrated 75 years of community service. To commemorate our special year, Mrs. Bush presented a speech on children's literacy to a sold out audience at Northwestern University.

Applecog

Contributed by Virginia Madsen. Virginia Madsen received
several acting awards along with an Academy Award Nomination for her
2004 performance in the motion picture, Sideways. Ms. Madsen is an
alumna of New Trier High School in Winnetka.

¾ cup butter

1 (16-ounce) package graham
crackers, crushed

⅔ cup packed brown sugar

2 teaspoons cinnamon

1 pint whipping cream

3 tablespoons sugar

1 teaspoon vanilla

1 (24-ounce) jar cinnamon
flavored applesauce

Melt butter over low heat. Stir in cracker crumbs, brown sugar and
cinnamon until slightly toasted, being careful not to burn the crumbs. Cool
to room temperature. Beat cream, sugar and vanilla until soft peaks form.
Set aside. Spread a layer of crumb mixture on the bottom of a 2-quart
serving bowl. Spoon a layer of applesauce over crumbs. Repeat layers to
halfway up side of bowl. Spread a layer of whipped cream reserving 1 cup.
Repeat layering crumb mixture and applesauce. Top with reserved cream.
Refrigerate several hours.

Yield: 4 to 6 servings

Mom's Pecan Cake

Contributed by Liz Phair, singer and songwriter.

Award-winning singer/songwriter Liz Phair grew up in Winnetka and attended New Trier High School. Ms. Phair's music is commonly at the top of music ranking lists and has been featured in major motion pictures. Her mother, Nancy, is a sustaining member of our League.

- CAKE -

9 egg yolks
1½ cups sugar
Pinch of salt

1½ cups finely ground pecans
12 egg whites

Preheat oven to 350 degrees. Butter three 8-inch round cake pans. Line each with wax paper and butter again. In a large mixing bowl, cream egg yolks, sugar and salt. Stir in pecans. In a separate bowl, beat egg whites until stiff peaks form. Fold egg whites into yolk mixture and spoon into prepared pans. Bake 40 to 50 minutes; cool layers on racks.

- CUSTARD FILLING -

3 egg yolks, lightly beaten
½ cup sugar
½ cup milk

2 ounces bittersweet chocolate
1 cup salted butter, softened

In top of a double boiler, combine egg yolks, sugar, milk and chocolate. Cook over medium heat until thickened, stirring often. Remove from heat and allow to cool. In a medium bowl, cream butter well. Gradually add custard mixture, blending well. Spread Custard Filling between layers and smooth over top of cake.

Yield: 8 servings

Braised Bosc Pears with Almond Torte, Tahitian Vanilla Gelato and Port Wine Sauce

Contributed by Lovells of Lake Forest.

- BRAISED PEARS -

¼ cup unsalted butter

2 Bosc pears, peeled, cut in half lengthwise, removing core

3 tablespoons sugar

½ vanilla bean

¾ cup port wine

Melt the butter in an 8-inch ovenproof skillet. Place pears flat side down in pan. Sprinkle with sugar. Remove seeds from the vanilla bean and add seeds to pears. Discard vanilla pod. Remove from heat and add half the port wine. Return to heat being careful of a flame up. Reduce liquid until almost dry. Add remaining port wine. Bake at 350 degrees until the pears become tender and caramelized. Add a little port during the braising process so the pears will not burn. Keep braised pears and sauce warm.

- ALMOND TORTE -

1 (9-ounce) package almonds, toasted

1 cup butter, cut into cubes

1 cup sugar

3 ounces all-purpose flour

6 large eggs

3 Bosh pears, diced

Place almonds, butter, sugar and flour in a food processor. Process while adding eggs, one at a time. Scrape sides of bowl and continue to process until smooth. Layer pears in a buttered and floured parchment paper-lined 10-inch baking dish. Spread almond mixture in pan, removing air bubbles. Bake at 350 degrees or until toothpick comes out clean. Using a 3-inch ring mold, punch out 4 tortes and set aside.

- PORT WINE SAUCE -

1 (750-milliliter) bottle port wine

⅓ cup sugar

½ vanilla bean, scrape out seeds

1 tablespoon cornstarch

3 tablespoons cold water

Combine port wine, sugar and vanilla seeds. Reduce to one-half cup. Dissolve cornstarch in cold water. Whisk in up to one tablespoon cornstarch mixture and briefly bring to a boil. Reduce heat to simmer and stir until thickened. If too thick, add a little water. Set aside.

- TO ASSEMBLE -

Tahitian Vanilla Gelato   powdered sugar

Arrange a braised pear, almond torte wedge dusted with powdered sugar and a 2 ounce scoop of Tahitian vanilla gelato on dessert plates. Spoon wine sauce on plate, over pear and torte. Dust with powdered sugar.

Yield: 4 servings

Vanilla Tropical Fruit Flan
with Tequila Caramel Sauce

Contributed by Nielsen-Massey Vanillas, Inc. located in Waukegan.

- COATING CARAMEL -

1 cup sugar   ½ cup orange juice

Cook sugar and juice over medium heat, scraping down
sides of pan with a rubber spatula to avoid crystallization.
Stir occasionally until it reaches a deep brown color.
Spread caramel to cover entire bottom of a flan mold. Set aside.

- TROPICAL FRUIT FLAN -

1 cup heavy cream
1 (32-ounce) can evaporated milk
2 Nielsen-Massey Tahitian
Vanilla Beans, split and scraped,
reserving vanilla bean pods
1 cinnamon stick
5 eggs

2 egg yolks
½ (14-ounce) can sweetened
condensed milk
½ cup coconut milk
½ cup mamey fruit purée
½ cup mango purée

Combine heavy cream, evaporated milk, vanilla beans, one vanilla pod
and cinnamon stick in a saucepan. Bring to boil. Reduce heat and simmer
a few minutes to infuse the milk. In a metal bowl, whisk together eggs, egg
yolks and sweetened condensed milk. Temper egg mixture with heavy
cream mixture then combine the two mixtures together. In a food processor,
blend coconut milk, mamey fruit and mango. Whisk fruit purée into egg
mixture and until well blended. Pour custard into flan mold. Cover with foil.
Place flan pan in a baking dish and add hot water half way up the
side of flan pan. Bake at 325 degrees until top is set. Remove
custard from hot water and cool. Refrigerate until cold.

- CARAMEL SAUCE -

1 cup sugar	1½ cups heavy cream
juice of ½ lemon	¼ cup tequila
1 vanilla bean pod	chocolate curls for garnish
1⅓ cups water	

Combine sugar, juice and scraped vanilla bean pod. Cook over medium heat until golden browned. Remove from heat and very slowly add cream, whisking constantly. Return to low heat and simmer 2 minutes. Add tequila and cook an additional 5 minutes. Unmold flan by running the tip of a knife around the edge of the flan. Invert onto a large round platter. Let caramel run out as much as possible. Place a slice of the flan on a serving plate. Top with tequila caramel sauce and sprinkle with chocolate curls.

Yield: 8 servings

Strawberry Shortcake

Contributed by Lili Taylor. Lili Taylor is an award-wining motion picture actress internationally recognized for her roles in such films as The Haunting, High Fidelity and Say Anything. Ms. Taylor grew up in Glencoe and attended New Trier High School in Winnetka.

- STRAWBERRIES -

3 (1-pint) packages strawberries, hulled and sliced

3 tablespoons sugar

2 tablespoons thinly sliced fresh mint

2 tablespoons Grand Marnier (optional)

Combine strawberries, sugar, mint and Grand Marnier. Gently mix to coat. Set aside.

- CREAM TOPPING -

½ cup sliced strawberries

1 cup cold whipping cream

1 teaspoon vanilla

¼ cup sugar

Purée strawberries and press through cheesecloth or sieve to remove seeds. Combine strawberry purée, cream, vanilla and sugar. Whip until soft peaks form. For sweeter cream, add more sugar. Keep refrigerated.

- BISCUITS -

1¾ cups all-purpose flour

4 tablespoons sugar

1 tablespoon baking powder

¼ teaspoon salt

¼ cup cold unsalted butter, cut into ½-inch pieces

1 cup cold whipping cream

1 tablespoon orange zest

2 tablespoons cold whipping cream

1 tablespoon sugar

mint leaves and sliced strawberries for garnish

Combine flour, sugar, baking powder and salt in a food processor. Blend 5 seconds. Add butter. Pulse on/off until crumbly. Add cream and zest. Process just until moist clumps form. Gather dough into a ball. Gently knead 5 times. Roll dough on a floured surface to 3/4 -inch thick. Using a 3-inch cutter, cut three biscuits. Re-roll dough and cut three more biscuits. Place on a parchment paper-lined baking sheet. Brush with cream and sprinkle with sugar. Bake at 375 degrees 20 minutes or until a pale golden color. Cool 15 minutes. May make 2 hours in advance. To assemble, cut biscuits in half horizontally. Place biscuit bottom in each of six bowls. Top each with berries and topping. Place each biscuit top over topping. Garnish with mint leaves and a sliced strawberry, fanned over biscuit.

Yield: 6 servings

Chocolate Raspberry Burritos

Contributed by Backyard Barbecue Store, Wilmette.

1 package 9-inch flour tortillas
1 pint fresh raspberries, rinsed
and patted dry

1 (12-ounce) package
chocolate chips
1/2 cup melted butter
Cinnamon sugar, to taste

Spread tortillas on a flat surface. Place a row of raspberries on the lower third of each; place a row of chocolate chips above and below the raspberries. Roll tortillas into burritos and wrap in foil. Refrigerate for at least 1 hour, allowing them to shape nicely.

Preheat grill to medium heat. Unwrap burritos and brush each with melted butter on all sides. Place burritos on the grill and brown 3 to 4 minutes on each side. Brush again with melted butter and sprinkle with cinnamon sugar as they are removed from grill and plated.

Lemon Almond Pound Cake

Contributed by Song O' Sixpence Specialty Foods and Catering, Winnetka.

4½ cups all-purpose flour

1 tablespoon baking powder

½ teaspoon baking soda

½ teaspoon salt

1½ cups butter, softened

3 cups sugar

6 eggs

zest of 3 lemons

juice of 3 lemons

1¼ cups milk

3 cups sliced almonds

Sift together flour, baking powder, baking soda and salt. Cream butter and sugar until fluffy. Add eggs one at a time, beating well after each addition. Combine zest, juice and milk. Add flour mixture alternately with milk mixture to creamed mixture until well combined. Fold in almonds. Pour batter into three buttered and floured 9 x 5-inch loaf pans. Bake at 350 degrees 35 to 45 minutes or until toothpick comes out clean.

Yield: 2 to 3 large loaves

One medium lemon equals approximately
1 tablespoon of lemon zest and
2 tablespoons of lemon juice.

Fudge

Contributed by Illinois Congresswoman, Jan Schakowsky,
and her daughter, Tillie Danoff.

1¾ cups sugar

2 heaping tablespoons
unsweetened cocoa powder

1 (5-ounce) can evaporated milk

¼ cup high quality butter

1 (6-ounce) package semi-sweet
chocolate chips

Combine sugar and cocoa in a saucepan. Add milk. Bring to boil.
Cook on medium heat 4 minutes, stirring constantly to avoid scorching. Stir
in butter and chocolate chips until smooth. Pour mixture into
9 x 9 x 2-inch baking dish. Cool.

Yield: 6 to 8 servings

Cappuccino Brownies

The aroma of baking brownies is irresistible, but well worth the wait when you savor these. The brownies are fantastic without the frosting but adding the frosting makes these the most delectable rich brownies ever.

- BROWNIES -

2 tablespoons instant espresso powder

8 ounces bittersweet chocolate, chopped

¾ cup unsalted butter, cut into pieces

1½ cups sugar

2 teaspoons vanilla

4 eggs

1 cup all-purpose flour

½ teaspoon salt

1 cup walnuts, chopped

Dissolve espresso powder in 1 tablespoon boiling water. Place a metal bowl over a pan of simmering water. Add espresso mixture, chocolate and butter. Stir until mixture is smooth. Remove from heat and cool to lukewarm. Stir in sugar and vanilla. Add eggs, one at a time, stirring well after each addition. Add flour and salt. Mix until just combined. Add walnuts. Pour batter into a buttered and floured 13 x 9 x 2-inch baking dish. Smooth top. Bake at 350 degrees 22 to 25 minutes or until toothpick comes out clean. Cool completely in pan on a rack.

- CREAM CHEESE FROSTING -

1 (8-ounce) package cream cheese, softened

⅜ cup unsalted butter, softened

1 teaspoon cinnamon

1½ cups powdered sugar

1 teaspoon vanilla

Beat cream cheese and butter until light and fluffy. Add cinnamon, powdered sugar and vanilla. Beat until smooth. Spread frosting over brownie layer. Refrigerate 1 hour or until firm.

- GLAZE -

1½ tablespoons instant espresso powder

6 ounces bittersweet chocolate

⅛ cup unsalted butter

½ cup heavy cream

Dissolve espresso powder in 1 tablespoon boiling water. Place a metal bowl over a pan of simmering water. Add espresso mixture, chocolate, butter and cream. Stir until smooth. Remove from heat. Cool to room temperature. Spread glaze over frosting layer. Cover and refrigerate at least 3 hours or overnight. Cut brownies while cold with a sharp knife. Serve cold or room temperature. Store covered and refrigerated.

Yield: 24 brownies

Having a dinner party and don't have the time to make a dessert? Serve high quality coffee ice cream in your nicest teacups. Add a little whipped cream and cocoa powder, and you have a lovely frozen cappuccino.

Brownies with Cream Cheese Swirl

The plate will be empty before you know it. A delight for kids and adults alike.

- CREAM CHEESE SWIRL -

1 (3-ounce) package cream cheese, softened

1/8 cup butter, softened

1/4 cup sugar

1 large egg

1 tablespoon all-purpose flour

1/2 teaspoon vanilla

Beat cream cheese and butter until light and fluffy. Gradually add sugar and beat well. Beat in egg. Stir in flour and vanilla. Set aside.

- BROWNIES -

6 (1-ounce) squares semi-sweet baking chocolate, chopped

3 tablespoons butter, softened

1/2 cup sugar

2 large eggs or egg substitute

1/2 cup all-purpose flour

1/2 teaspoon baking powder

1/4 teaspoon salt

2 teaspoons vanilla

1/4 teaspoon almond extract

1 cup semi-sweet chocolate chips

1/4 cup chopped nuts (optional)

Combine chocolate and butter in a heavy small saucepan. Cook and stir until smooth. Cool slightly. In a separate bowl, beat sugar and eggs 2 minutes until slightly thickened. Mix in flour, baking powder and salt. Stir in chocolate mixture, vanilla and almond extract. Add chocolate chips and nuts. Spread half the chocolate batter into a lightly buttered and floured 8 x 8 x 2-inch square baking dish. Spread cream cheese mixture over batter. Spoon remaining chocolate batter on top. Using the tip of a knife, gently swirl through batter making a marble design. Bake at 350 degrees 30 minutes or until toothpick comes out clean. Cool in pan on a rack. Cut into squares.

Yield: 8 to 10 servings

Peanut Butter Oatmeal Cookies

Finding the perfect peanut butter cookie recipe is not always easy.
This foolproof recipe is an ideal after school treat with vanilla ice cream.

1 cup butter, softened	1 cup all-purpose flour
1 cup packed brown sugar	$\frac{1}{2}$ teaspoon salt
1 cup sugar	2 teaspoons baking soda
2 eggs	2 cups dry quick oats
1 teaspoon vanilla	$\frac{1}{2}$ cup butterscotch chips
1 cup creamy peanut butter	

Cream butter, brown sugar and sugar. Beat in eggs and vanilla.
Stir in peanut butter. Mix well. Add flour, salt, baking soda and oats.
Mix in butterscotch chips. Drop dough by rounded teaspoons onto baking
sheet. Press flat with a floured fork in a crisscross pattern.
Bake at 350 degrees 10 to 12 minutes.

Yield: 4 to 5 dozen cookies

When baking with baking soda or baking powder,
make a solution with a teaspoon of water and the powders.
In liquid form, the baking powders are much more
evenly distributed through the dough.

Angel Cookies

Nothing but simple and delicious! This is one you won't want to miss.

3 egg whites	1 (6-ounce) package semi-sweet
3/4 cup sugar	chocolate chips
1 teaspoon vanilla	1/2 cup chopped nuts (optional)

Beat egg whites until soft peaks form. Slowly add sugar while beating. When stiff peaks form, gently stir in vanilla, chocolate chips and nuts. Drop dough by teaspoonfuls onto greased baking sheets. Bake at 250 degrees 25 to 35 minutes. Cool on wire racks.

Yield: 36 to 40 cookies

Egg whites will beat faster
and higher if you add a pinch of salt.

Lemon Meltaways

Heavenly!

- COOKIES -

1¼ cups all-purpose flour   ¾ cup butter, softened

½ cup cornstarch   1 teaspoon lemon zest

⅓ cup powdered sugar   1 tablespoon lemon juice

Blend flour, cornstarch, powdered sugar, butter, zest and juice. Divide dough in half. Shape each half into an 8 x 1-inch roll. Wrap in plastic wrap. Refrigerate 1 to 2 hours until firm. Slice dough and bake at 350 degrees 8 to 12 minutes.

- FROSTING -

¾ cup powdered sugar   1 teaspoon lemon zest

¼ cup butter, softened   1 teaspoon lemon juice

Blend powdered sugar, butter, zest and juice. Frost cooled cookies.

Yield: 2 to 3 dozen cookies

Melting Moments

These will be gobbled up fast.
These light and creamy delicacies melt in your mouth.

1 cup butter, softened	3/4 cup cornstarch
1/3 cup powdered sugar	1 teaspoon vanilla
1 cup all-purpose flour	

Cream butter, powdered sugar, flour, cornstarch and vanilla.
Drop dough by teaspoonfuls onto baking sheet. Bake at 350 degrees
10 to 15 minutes or until lightly browned.

- FROSTING -

1 cup powdered sugar	1 teaspoon vanilla
1/8 cup butter, melted	whipping cream

Blend powdered sugar, butter and vanilla. Add whipping cream
to reach spreading consistency. May add food coloring to match
holiday season. Spread frosting over cooled cookies.

Yield: 2 to 3 dozen cookies

Raspberry Bar Cookies

Super to bring to a picnic.

½ cup butter, softened
½ cup packed light brown sugar
1 cup all-purpose flour
¼ teaspoon baking soda

⅛ teaspoon salt
1 cup quick oats
¾ cup seedless raspberry jam

Cream butter and brown sugar. Add flour, baking soda, salt and oats. Press 2 cups mixture into the bottom of a buttered 8 x 8 x 2-inch baking dish. Spread the jam to within ¼-inch of the edge. Sprinkle remaining crumb mixture on top and lightly press it into jam. Bake at 350 degrees 35 to 40 minutes. Cool on a wire rack before cutting into 2 x 1½-inch bars.

Yield: 20 bars

Caramel Pecan Triangles

These cookies are a big hit at our
JLE-NS Sustainers' Soups and Sweets Holiday Party.

1 cup packed light brown sugar

3/4 cup unsalted butter, melted

2 large eggs

1 teaspoon vanilla

1 teaspoon bourbon (optional)

1/2 cup all-purpose flour

1/2 cup cocoa powder

1/2 teaspoon salt

3/4 cup unsalted butter

1/2 cup dark corn syrup

3 cups packed light brown sugar

1/2 teaspoon salt

2/3 cup whipping cream

2 tablespoons vanilla

3 1/2 cups pecan pieces, toasted

Line a 13 x 9 x 2-inch baking dish with foil. Grease foil. Beat brown sugar, butter, eggs, vanilla and bourbon until smooth. Combine flour, cocoa and salt. Gradually add to creamed mixture. Spread mixture into prepared pan. Bake at 375 degrees 15 minutes. Combine butter, syrup, brown sugar and salt in a saucepan. Bring to boil, stirring constantly, until mixture reaches hard ball stage or candy thermometer reaches 250 degrees. Remove from heat. Stir in whipping cream and vanilla. Add pecans. Pour over crust. Bake at 375 degrees 25 minutes. Cool on a rack. Refrigerate 8 hours. Cut into 12 squares. Cut each square into two triangles. Store in the refrigerator.

Yield: 2 dozen

Pistachio Biscotti with Cranberries

Slightly salty and sweet, these are great around Thanksgiving and Christmas.

2¼ cups all-purpose flour

1½ teaspoons baking powder

¾ teaspoon salt

⅜ cup unsalted butter, softened

¾ cup sugar

2 large eggs

1 tablespoon lemon zest

1½ teaspoons vanilla

1 teaspoon aniseed

1 cup dried cranberries

¾ cup shelled pistachios

Line three baking sheets with parchment paper. Sift together flour, baking powder and salt. In a separate bowl, beat butter and sugar until smooth. Beat in eggs, one at a time. Add zest, vanilla and aniseed. Beat in flour mixture just until blended. Stir in cranberries and pistachios. Turn dough onto lightly floured surface. Divide dough in half. Roll each half into a 15-inch long log. Flatten slightly to about 1½-inches wide. Transfer each log to baking sheet, spaced 3-inches apart. Bake at 325 degrees 28 minutes. They should be almost firm to touch yet still pale. Cool 10 minutes. Transfer to a cutting board. Using a serrated knife, gently cut crosswise into ½-inch thick diagonal slices. Place cut side down on baking sheet. Bake 9 minutes, turn and bake an additional 9 minutes. Cool and serve. May be made up to 5 days in advance and stored in an airtight container.

Yield: 40 biscotti

Working with floury dough? Don't flour your hands.
It's true the flour will keep the dough from sticking to your fingers; however, it can also add too much flour to the mixture causing over dry dough. Instead, oil your hands with a little olive oil. Not only will the dough keep from sticking, but also your hands will get the benefit of a natural moisturizer!

Milk Chocolate Florentine Cookies

Delicate and delicious, these are very special.

⅔ cup butter	¼ cup milk
2 cups quick oats	1 teaspoon vanilla
1 cup sugar	¼ teaspoon salt
⅔ cup all-purpose flour	1 (12-ounce) package milk chocolate chips
¼ cup corn syrup	

Melt butter over low heat. Remove from heat. Stir in oats, sugar, flour, syrup, milk, vanilla and salt. Mix well. Drop dough by teaspoonfuls about 3-inches apart onto foil lined baking sheet. Spread thin with rubber spatula. Bake at 375 degrees 5 to 7 minutes. Cool on baking sheet. Peel foil away from cookies. Melt chocolate chips in the top of a double boiler. Stir until smooth. Spread chocolate on flat side of half of cookies. Top with remaining cookies.

Yield: 3½ dozen cookies

Effortless Chocolate Gâteau

Serve warm with fresh cream and sprinkle cinnamon on top.

½ cup butter	2 eggs
2 squares unsweetened chocolate	½ teaspoon vanilla
1 cup sugar	¼ cup all-purpose flour
	¼ teaspoon salt

Melt butter and chocolate. Remove from heat and cool. Add sugar, eggs and vanilla. Mix well. Stir in flour and salt. Pour batter into a buttered and floured 8 x 8 x 2-inch baking dish. Bake at 325 degrees 20 to 25 minutes. Serve warm.

Yield: 6 to 8 servings

Ancho Chile Devil's Food Cake

A winning combination of chile and chocolate makes this an interesting alternative to the usual chocolate cake. Serve it with a fine vanilla ice cream topped with a dash of cinnamon for an excellent dessert.

- GANACHE -

1 (6-ounce) package semi-sweet chocolate chips

¾ cup heavy cream

Place chocolate in a small bowl. Scald cream over medium heat. Pour over chocolate and stir until smooth. Let stand until slightly thickened. Ganache should be spreading consistency but able to pour.

- CAKE -

1¼ cups cake flour

½ cup unsweetened cocoa powder

3 tablespoons ancho chile powder

⅛ teaspoon cayenne pepper

1 teaspoon baking soda

¼ teaspoon baking powder

½ teaspoon salt

⅔ cup unsalted butter, softened

1½ cups sugar

3 large eggs, room temperature

1 teaspoon vanilla

½ cup buttermilk, room temperature

½ cup hot coffee

Lightly spray two 9-inch cake pans. Line pans with disks of parchment paper or greased wax paper. Sift together flour, cocoa, chile powder, cayenne, baking soda, baking powder and salt. Sift twice to aerate. Beat butter and sugar at high speed until smooth. Add eggs, one at a time. Beat 5 minutes until light and fluffy. Fold in one-third flour mixture. Add vanilla, half the buttermilk and half the coffee. Beat in second one-third flour mixture. Fold in remaining buttermilk and coffee. Add remaining flour mixture. Divide batter between two pans. Bake at 350 degrees 30 minutes or until center springs back. Cool in pans on a wire rack. Invert each cake onto a plate. Trim top with a serrated knife if necessary. Spread one-third ganache over one cake layer. Top with second cake layer. Frost top and sides with remaining ganache.

Yield: 10 to 12 servings

Pumpkin Cheesecake

This cheesecake gets rave reviews.

- CRUST -

¾ cup gingersnap crumbs

¾ cup graham cracker crumbs

¼ cup sugar

¼ cup butter, softened

Combine gingersnap crumbs, cracker crumbs, sugar and butter until crumbly. Press mixture onto bottom and sides of a well buttered 9-inch springform pan. Refrigerate at least 30 minutes.

- FILLING -

4 (8-ounce) packages cream cheese, softened

1½ cups sugar

⅓ cup all-purpose flour, sifted

1½ teaspoons cinnamon

1 teaspoon grated nutmeg

1 teaspoon ground cloves

¼ teaspoon ground allspice

⅛ teaspoon salt

6 eggs

1 (16-ounce) can pumpkin purée

Beat cream cheese, sugar, flour, cinnamon, nutmeg, cloves, allspice, salt and eggs until smooth. Beat in pumpkin until smooth. Pour filling into crust. Bake at 325 degrees 1 hour, 30 minutes. Turn off the oven and leave cake in oven 30 minutes with door ajar. Transfer to a wire rack and cool completely.

- TOPPING -

1 cup heavy cream	⅛ teaspoon cinnamon
1 teaspoon sugar	½ cup chopped pecans
1 teaspoon vanilla	

Whip cream in a chilled bowl with sugar, vanilla and cinnamon until soft peaks form. Spread topping over cake. Sprinkle with nuts. Transfer to a serving platter.

Yield: 12 to 15 servings

Keep powdered sugar in a
shaker ready to garnish desserts.

Rum Cake

This is a wonderfully moist cake.

- HOT RUM GLAZE -

¼ cup water   ¼ cup light rum
½ cup butter   1 cup sugar

Combine water, butter, rum and sugar in a saucepan.
Heat to boiling. Boil 3 minutes. Keep glaze hot.

- CAKE -

1 (18-ounce) package   ½ cup light rum
yellow cake mix   ½ cup vegetable oil
1 (3-ounce) package instant
vanilla pudding mix   4 eggs
½ cup warm water   whipped topping

Beat cake mix, pudding mix, water, rum, oil and eggs until smooth.
Pour batter into a well greased Bundt pan. Bake at 325 degrees 50 to
60 minutes. Pour hot glaze over hot cake while in pan. Let stand 1 hour.
Invert onto a serving platter. Serve warm with whipped topping.

Yield: 12 to 15 servings

Banana Cake

This is possibly one of the best sheet cakes
in the world and ideal for taking to the office or a party.

¾ cup butter, softened
3 cups sugar
4 eggs, room temperature
1 (8-ounce) container sour cream
4 ripe bananas, mashed
3 cups sifted cake flour

pinch of salt
½ teaspoon baking powder
½ teaspoon baking soda
2 teaspoons vanilla
1 cup nuts, walnut or pecans

Cream butter and sugar. Add eggs, one at a time, until blended.
Stir in sour cream and bananas. Add flour, salt, baking powder and baking
soda. Stir in vanilla and nuts. Pour batter into a 13 x 9 x 2-inch baking dish.
Bake at 350 degrees 50 minutes. Cool completely.

- CREAM CHEESE FROSTING -

1 (3-ounce) package
cream cheese, softened
⅜ cup butter, softened

2 cups powdered sugar
1 teaspoon heavy cream or milk
1 teaspoon vanilla

Blend cream cheese and butter until smooth. Stir in powdered sugar.
Add milk and vanilla. Mix well. Spread frosting over cake.

Yield: 12 to 15 servings

Triple Lemon Cake

A perfect lemon cake that is worth the effort.
No time to make the cake? The curd is fantastic with scones.

- LEMON CAKE -

1¼ cups sugar	2 tablespoons lemon juice
zest of 2 lemons	1¾ cups cake flour
3 eggs	2 teaspoons baking powder
¾ cup unsalted butter, softened	¾ teaspoon baking soda
¾ cup sour cream	¾ teaspoon salt
¼ cup plus 2 tablespoons orange juice	

Mince sugar and zest in food processor until very fine. Add eggs and process 1 minute. Add butter and process one minute more. Add sour cream, orange juice and lemon juice. Mix well. Sift together flour, baking powder, baking soda and salt. Stir flour mixture into batter just until combined. Do not over mix. Butter three 8-inch pans, line with parchment paper and butter again. Divide batter among the pans. Bake at 350 degrees 20 minutes. Cool 10 minutes on wire racks. Remove from pans and cool completely.

- LEMON CURD -

⅔ cup sugar	½ cup lemon juice
zest of 1 lemon	pinch of salt
5 egg yolks	½ cup butter, melted and hot

Mince sugar and zest in food processor until very fine. Add egg yolks, juice and salt and process. With machine running, pour hot butter through the feed tube. Transfer mixture to a saucepan. Cook over low heat, stirring constantly, until thickened. Do not boil. Cool, cover and refrigerate. Reserve 2 tablespoons for Icing.

- LEMON ICING -

3½ cups powdered sugar   4 to 5 tablespoons sour cream

zest of 2 lemons   ⅓ cup unsalted butter

pinch of salt   2 tablespoons Lemon Curd

Mince powdered sugar and zest in food processor until very fine. Stir in salt, sour cream, butter and lemon curd. Refrigerate 15 minutes. If icing is too thin, add more powdered sugar. To assemble, spread bottom and middle layers of cake with Lemon Curd. Cover top and sides of the cake with Lemon Icing. Garnish with edible flowers or fresh fruit slices.

Yield: 12 servings

Keep oranges and lemons on hand for garnish.

Italian Cream Cake

This is an elegant cake that is well worth the effort.
Perfect for a bridal shower.

- CAKE -

2 cups sugar	2 cups all-purpose flour
½ cup butter, softened	1 teaspoon baking soda
½ cup vegetable shortening	2 cups buttermilk
1 teaspoon vanilla	1 (3½-ounce) can flaked coconut
2 egg yolks	5 egg whites, stiffly beaten

Cream sugar, butter, shortening and vanilla. Add egg yolks, one at a time, until blended. Combine flour and baking soda. Add flour mixture alternately with buttermilk to creamed mixture. Fold in coconut. Fold in egg whites until mixed. Divide batter among three 9-inch cake pans. Bake at 350 degrees 25 minutes. Cool completely.

- ITALIAN CREAM CHEESE FROSTING -

1 (8-ounce) package cream cheese, softened	3 (16-ounce) packages powdered sugar
1 cup butter, softened	4 teaspoons vanilla
	5 cups pecan halves

Beat cream cheese and butter until light and fluffy. Beat in powdered sugar. Stir in vanilla. Frost between cake layers, top and outer cake with either Italian Cream Cheese Frosting or Fluffy White Frosting. Garnish with pecans, fresh strawberries or edible flowers.

- FLUFFY WHITE FROSTING -

2 cups sugar ⅛ teaspoon salt

⅔ cup water 5 egg whites

2 tablespoons light corn syrup 6 teaspoons vanilla

3 teaspoons cream of tartar

Combine sugar, water, corn syrup, cream of tartar and salt in a heavy saucepan. Bring to boil, stirring constantly. Cook without stirring until mixture reaches soft ball stage or candy thermometer reaches 240 degrees. Beat egg whites until soft peaks form. Slowly add hot syrup, beating constantly. Add vanilla and beat 5 to 7 minutes until soft peaks form and frosting is spreading consistency.

Yield: 12 to 15 servings

Divine Chocolate Cake

Rich and dense. This chocolate cake is the perfect finale to any meal.

3 (1-ounce) squares unsweetened chocolate, chopped

1 (8¼ -ounce) can julienned beets

½ cup unsalted butter, softened, room temperature

2½ cups firmly packed brown sugar

3 large eggs, room temperature

2 teaspoons vanilla

2-cups all-purpose flour

2 teaspoons baking soda

½ teaspoon salt

½ cup buttermilk

Melt chocolate in a double boiler over hot water. Set aside to cool. Drain beet juice into a small bowl, reserving juice. Dice beets into very small pieces. Add to beet juice and set aside. Beat butter, brown sugar, eggs and vanilla 5 minutes until fluffy. Reduce to low speed and beat in melted chocolate. Combine flour, baking soda and salt. On low speed, add flour mixture alternately with buttermilk into chocolate mixture, beginning and ending with flour. Add beets and juice. Beat 1 minute until blended. The batter will be thin and the beets will be visible. Divide batter between two greased and floured 9-inch cake pans. Bake at 350 degrees 30 to 35 minutes or until toothpick comes out clean. Do not overbake or the cake will be too dry. Cool cake completely, overnight is ideal.

- FUDGE FROSTING -

2 cups whipping cream

1 pound semi-sweet chocolate, chopped

2 teaspoons vanilla

Heat cream in a saucepan just until a boiling. Remove from heat. Add chocolate and vanilla, stirring until chocolate melts and is smooth. Transfer mixture to a glass or plastic bowl (not metal). Refrigerate 50 to 60 minutes, stirring every 10 minutes until mixture thickens like pudding. At this point, frosting will begin to set very quickly. Keep in refrigerator and stir every

5 minutes until frosting is thick like fudge. To assemble, place one cake layer top-side down on serving platter. Spread with one-third frosting. Top with second cake layer with bottom side up. Spread remaining frosting over top and sides. Let stand at room temperature to set frosting. Frosted cake may be stored at room temperature, uncovered, overnight or refrigerated for up to two days. Bring to room temperature before serving.

Yield: 10 to 12 servings

Mixed Berry Crisp
For a little extra decadence, pour heavy cream on top.

2 (12-ounce) packages frozen mixed berries, thawed

¼ cup sugar

1 cup all-purpose flour

1 tablespoon lemon juice

¾ cup all-purpose flour

¾ cup dry quick oats

⅔ cup packed brown sugar

1 teaspoon cinnamon

½ teaspoon ground ginger

¼ teaspoon ground nutmeg

¼ teaspoon salt

½ cup cold butter, cut into pieces

Combine berries, sugar, flour and juice tossing to coat. Transfer to a 9-inch glass pie plate. Mix together flour, oats, brown sugar, cinnamon, ginger, nutmeg and salt. Cut in butter until crumbly. Sprinkle over berries. Bake at 375 degrees 1 hour until bubbly and golden browned. Let stand 15 minutes. Serve warm or room temperature.

Yield: 6 servings

All-Year-Round Cobbler

An All-American classic.

- SPRING/SUMMER VARIATION -

⅓ cup butter

1 cup sugar

1 cup all-purpose flour

1 teaspoon baking powder

¾ cup milk

1 pint fruit, blueberries, peeled and chopped peaches, cherries, strawberries or combination

vanilla ice cream

Melt butter and pour into 13 x 9 x 2-inch baking dish. Beat together sugar, flour, baking powder and milk. Pour batter over butter. Scatter fruit over batter. Bake at 375 degrees 45 to 60 minutes or until bubbly and golden browned. Serve warm with ice cream.

- FALL/WINTER VARIATION -

⅓ cup butter

1 cup sugar

1 cup all-purpose flour

1 teaspoon baking powder

1 teaspoon cinnamon

¾ cup milk

3 cups peeled and cubed Granny Smith apples

30 caramel candies, unwrapped

2 tablespoons half-and-half

vanilla ice cream

Melt butter and pour into bottom of a 13 x 9 x 2-inch baking dish. Beat together sugar, flour, baking powder, cinnamon and milk. Pour batter over butter. Scatter apples over batter. Bake at 375 degrees 45 to 60 minutes or until bubbly and golden browned. Place caramels and half-and-half in a micro safe bowl. Heat 1 minute and stir. Repeat until sauce is smooth. Serve warm cobbler with caramel sauce and ice cream.

Yield: 6 to 8 servings

Baked Pears in Rosemary Maple Custard

The aroma of the rosemary is intoxicating. Use ripe pears for the best results.

4 medium, ripe, Bartlett pears	2 tablespoons all-purpose flour
1 cup pure maple syrup	½ teaspoon vanilla
4 sprigs fresh rosemary	⅛ teaspoon salt
1 tablespoon butter	½ cup heavy cream
2 large eggs	½ cup whole milk

Peel pears and cut in half. Scoop out cores and remove fiber from stem to core. Pour maple syrup into a 10-inch skillet. Place pears rounded side down in maple syrup with sprigs of rosemary between the pears. Simmer 5 minutes. Flip pears and cook an additional 5 minutes or until tender. Arrange pears facing down and stems facing inward in a buttered 9-inch round baking dish or 10-inch pie pan. Discard rosemary and pour syrup into a measuring cup. Syrup should have reduced to one-half cup, if not, place back in skillet and reduce. Whisk one egg with flour. Add second egg. Whisk in syrup, vanilla, salt, cream and milk. Pour batter over pears. Bake at 350 degrees 25 to 30 minutes or until custard has browned. Slice custard into wedges and serve.

Yield: 4 to 6 servings

Peach, Plum and Blackberry Cobbler

A colorful and popular summertime dessert.

6 peaches, peeled, pitted and sliced

2 red plums, halved, pitted and sliced

1½ pints blackberries or 1½ cups frozen, thawed

⅔ cup sugar

3 tablespoons quick tapioca

¾ cup all-purpose flour

1 teaspoon baking powder

¼ teaspoon salt

1 tablespoon sugar

1 teaspoon lemon zest

3 tablespoons cold butter

6 tablespoons cold whipping cream

3 tablespoons brown sugar

½ teaspoon cinnamon

¼ teaspoon ground ginger

pinch of ground cloves

2 tablespoons all-purpose flour

⅛ cup cold butter

Combine peaches, plums, blueberries, sugar and tapioca in an 8 x 8 x 2-inch baking dish. Toss to coat. Bake at 400 degrees 50 minutes until tender and bubbly. Cool 10 minutes. Combine flour, baking powder, salt and sugar in a bowl. Stir in zest and butter. Using fingers, mix until crumbly. Stir in cream until moist clumps form. Gather into a ball. With floured hands, shape dough into a 6-inch square. Cut into six equal triangles. Mix together brown sugar, cinnamon, ginger, cloves and flour. Cut in butter until crumbly. Place biscuits over hot fruit. Top with sugar mixture. Bake at 400 degrees 25 minutes until golden browned. Cool 30 minutes.

Yield: 6 servings

Apricot Whip with Berries

A light and lovely way to end a meal.

6 ounces dried apricots

1 cup orange juice

2 tablespoons honey

½ teaspoon vanilla

1 cup egg whites, about 8 large
eggs, room temperature

pinch of salt

1 cup sugar

2 pints mixed berries, hulled,
sliced and lightly sugared

Combine apricots, juice and honey in a saucepan. Cook 20 minutes
until tender. Transfer to food processor. Add vanilla and purée, scraping
down sides of bowl. Transfer to a large bowl and cool. May be made two
days in advance. Cover and refrigerate. Bring to room temperature before
continuing. Beat egg whites with salt until soft peaks form. Gradually add
sugar and beat until stiff. Fold into purée in two additions. Spoon mixture
into a greased 9 x 9 x 2-inch baking dish. Smooth the top. Place on a
baking sheet with sides. Pour water into sheet to ½-inch. Bake at 350
degrees 40 minutes until firm and golden browned. Cover with
foil if browning too quickly. Cool 15 minutes or up to 3 hours.
Spoon Apricot Whip into deep bowls. Serve with berries.

Yield: 6 servings

Cream will whip better if you add a pinch of salt.

Fresh Michigan Blueberry Pie

As gorgeous as it is delicious, this is a real treat during blueberry season.

2½ cups blueberries

⅛ teaspoon salt

¾ cup sugar

lemon zest

2 tablespoons cornstarch

1¼ cups water

2 tablespoons lemon juice

1 tablespoon butter

2½ cups blueberries

1 (9-inch) shortbread cookie pie crust

vanilla ice cream

Combine blueberries, salt, sugar and zest. Dissolve cornstarch with water. Stir cornstarch into berries. Cook and stir over low boil until mixture thickens. Remove from heat. Add juice and butter. Stir until butter melts. Cool. Fold in blueberries. Pour filling into crust. Refrigerate 4 hours or until firm. Serve with ice cream.

Yield: 8 servings

Summer Key Lime Pie

1 (14-ounce) can sweetened condensed milk

1 (8-ounce) container frozen whipped topping, thawed

⅓ cup Key lime juice

1 (9-inch) graham cracker crust

1 lime, thinly sliced

Blend milk, whipped topping and juice. Pour filling into pie crust. Top with lime slices. Freeze overnight. Defrost 30 minutes before serving.

Yield: 6 to 8 servings

Apple Cranberry Pie

The best of autumn in one bite.

1½ cups fresh or frozen cranberries, thawed
1¼ cups sugar
6 tablespoons all-purpose flour
1 tablespoon orange zest
1¼ teaspoons cinnamon
½ teaspoon ground nutmeg

¼ teaspoon salt
6 cups sliced Granny Smith apples
1 (10-inch) pie crust, unbaked
1 cup all-purpose flour
⅔ cup packed brown sugar
½ cup butter, cut into pieces

Sort, rinse and drain cranberries. Discard any bruised ones. Combine sugar, flour, zest, cinnamon, nutmeg and salt. Add cranberries and apples. Mix to coat. Pour filling into pie crust. Mix flour and brown sugar. Cut in butter until crumbly. Sprinkle over filling. Place pie plate on a baking sheet. Bake on bottom rack at 375 degrees 55 to 65 minutes. Check after 30 minutes and if browning quickly, cover loosely with foil. Cool on rack 2 hours, 30 minutes to 3 hours.

Yield: 8 servings

Mincemeat Cream Cheese Pie

Tastes like Christmas!

CRUST

1 cup sifted all-purpose flour	½ cup butter, softened
¼ cup sugar	1 egg yolk, slightly beaten
1 teaspoon lemon zest	¼ teaspoon vanilla

Combine flour, sugar and zest. Cut in butter with pastry blender or two knives until crumbly. Stir in egg yolk and vanilla. Mix with hands until well blended. Press evenly into a 9-inch pie plate making a small edge on rim. Bake at 400 degrees 10 minutes or until lightly browned. Cool on rack.

FILLING

1 (8-ounce) package cream cheese, softened	¼ teaspoon vanilla
2 eggs, slightly beaten	1 cup prepared mincemeat
⅓ cup sugar	1 cup sour cream

Beat cream cheese until light and fluffy. Add eggs, sugar and vanilla. Mix well. Spoon mincemeat into crust. Spread cheese mixture on top, smoothing out top. Bake at 350 degrees 25 to 30 minutes or until golden browned. Remove from oven. Top with sour cream. Cool on rack.

Yield: 8 servings

Easy Almond Torte

Add chocolate chips for a richer dessert.

1⅔ cups all-purpose flour

1½ cups sugar

1 cup butter, melted

⅛ teaspoon salt

2 tablespoons almond extract

2 eggs, beaten

1 (2¼-ounce) package sliced almonds

Combine flour, sugar, butter, salt, almond extract and eggs. Mix well. Pour filing into a greased 10-inch pie pan.

Sprinkle with almonds. Bake at 350 degrees 35 to 40 minutes.

Yield: 8 servings

When melting chocolate chips for decorating, seal them in a zipper sandwich bag and put in a pan of hot water. After a few minutes, knead the bag to smooth the chocolate, and then cut a small hole in a corner of the bag to pipe out the chocolate. You can leave the leftovers in the bag to cool, and then crumble for other uses.

Candy Shop Pizza

A fun activity for kids on a rainy afternoon.

1 (18-ounce) package refrigerated chocolate chip cookie dough

1 (6-ounce) package semi-sweet chocolate chips

1 cup creamy or chunky peanut butter

1 cup chopped assorted candies (Butterfingers, Nestle crunch bars, Baby Ruth, Goobers, Raisinets)

Press cookie dough evenly onto bottom of greased 12-inch pizza pan or 13 x 9 x 2-inch baking dish. Bake at 350 degrees 8 to 10 minutes until edge is set and center is still slightly soft. Do not over bake. Immediately sprinkle chocolate chips over hot crust and drop peanut butter by the spoonful onto chips. Let stand 5 minutes until chocolate melts. Place in oven if needed. Gently spread chocolate and peanut butter evenly over cookie crust. Sprinkle chopped candy in single layer over pizza. Cut into wedges and serve warm or at room temperature.

Yield: 12 servings

The first advertisement for jelly beans was published in the Chicago Daily News on July 5, 1905.

Play-Doh

Fun for kids. Although edible, not recommended for consumption.

1 cup salt	water
2 cups all-purpose flour	food coloring
2 tablespoons vegetable oil	zip-top plastic bags

Combine salt, flour and oil. Slowly add water. Knead mixture until doughy.
Divide mixture into portions. Add a few drops of food coloring.
Stir well. Store refrigerated.

Yield: 3 cups

To make a lava lamp, fill a glass with Club Soda and
drop in two raisins. The carbonation will cause the raisins to
repeatedly bob to the surface and they sink again.

Beverages

Market Square Fountain

- Lake Forest -

The History of Lake Forest

The City of Lake Forest was incorporated as a City in 1861 and was primarily founded to support the establishment of church-related educational institutions.

Lake Forest owes its beauty to the vision of landscape designer Almerin Hotchkiss. His 1857 plan for Lake Forest was based on picturesque principles worked out for English gardens and American parks.

Hotchkiss' general concept reflects the plan of the city in a park, with its street laid out in an organic, winding pattern. This plan takes into account many of the natural features in the area, such as the ravines and lake bluffs, instead of forcing the street plan into a formal gridiron plan.

In addition, Lake Forest is noted for the character of its architecture whether erected for residential, religious, educational or public purposes. Noted Lake Forest architects include Charles Frost and Howard Van Doren Shaw, both of whom also maintained estates. Even such well-known eastern architects as James Gamble Rogers and Charles Platt were called upon to design for Lake Forest clients. It is these same factors that give Lake Forest its historical significance that also make the estate areas of residential Lake Forest historically and visually distinctive.

4th of July Beach Bar B Q

The perfect menu to follow the traditional 4th of July Parade.

Southern Sweet Tea

Lemonade Mojitos

Sausage Bites in Bourbon Sauce on a Bed of Sweet Potatoes

Black Bean and Corn Salsa

Low Country Boil

Marinated Flank Steak

Redskin Potato Salad

Garden of Eden Vegetables

Fresh Michigan Blueberry Pie

Cranberry Mojito

Contributed by Mayor Mike Rummel, Lake Forest.

½ cup sugar
½ cup concentrated cranberry juice
1 cup rum

2 cups sparkling water
¼ cup ground fresh mint
mint sprigs and lemon slices for garnish

Blend sugar and cranberry juice. Add ice. Stir in rum. Top off with sparkling water. Coat the inside of tall thin glasses with mint. Pour juice mixture into glasses. Garnish with mint sprig and lemon slice.

Yield: 4 to 6 servings

Electric Lemonade

Recipe created by chef and best-selling author, Art Smith.
Delightfully dangerous, a summertime classic with a twist that is for adults only.

2 cups sugar
2 cups water
1 cup fresh lemon juice
1 large mint sprig, finely chopped

1 cup lemon-flavored vodka
splash of sparkling water
mint sprigs for garnish
1 tablespoon lemon zest for garnish

Heat sugar and water in a small saucepan. Boil 3 minutes to make simple syrup. Let cool. In medium bowl, stir together 1 cup syrup (leftover syrup can be refrigerated indefinitely), juice and half mint. Pour mixture into ice-cube tray and freeze for one hour. Combine frozen cubes, remaining mint, vodka and sparkling water in a blender. Process until smooth. Pour into chilled glasses. Garnish with mint sprigs and lemon zest.

Yield: 8 servings

Skylark

Contributed by Count Jan-Roman Potocki.

This cocktail, designed by Jerri Banks, was named after the legendary Arab stallion Skowronek (Polish for skylark). Later exported via England to the United States, his bloodline can be traced in many great American thoroughbred champions.

5 to 6 grape tomatoes
pinch of salt
3 to 4 basil leaves

1½ ounces Potocki Wódka
dash of balsamic vinegar

In a cobbler shaker bottom, muddle grape tomatoes and salt to remove liquid. Add all but one basil leaf and muddle until scent rises from shaker. Add vodka and ice. Shake well and strain into chilled cocktail glass. For garnish, place leaf atop cocktail and 1 to 2 drops of balsamic vinegar on leaf.

Yield: 1 serving

Easy Cranberry Margaritas

These are elegant during the holidays!

1½ cups cranberries
1¼ cups cranberry juice cocktail
¾ cup frozen limeade, thawed

¾ cup tequila
½ cup Grand Marnier
Coarsely crushed ice

Reserve 12 cranberries. Combine remaining cranberries, juice cocktail, limeade, tequila and Grand Marnier in a blender. Process until smooth. Add ice and blend until smooth. Pour some cranberry juice in a shallow bowl. Dip glass rims in juice and then in sugar. Pour mixture into glasses and garnish with cranberries.

Yield: 6 servings

Winter Warmer Coffees

Contributed by Spillin' the Beans in Wilmette.

- BLACKBERRY VIENNESE COFFEE -

2 shots espresso   1 ounce blackberry flavoring

1¾ cups steamed chocolate milk

Mix all ingredients and serve hot.

- CAPPUCCINO ROYALE -

2 shots espresso   ½ ounce each Amaretto,

1½ cups steamed milk   Bailey's and Triple Sec

Milk, for frothing

Combine espresso, steamed milk and liqueurs.
Pour in serving cups and top with frothed milk.

A shot is usually considered to be about 1½ ounces or 3 tablespoons.

Southern Sweet Tea

This is the real thing.

5 regular tea bags   1 cup sugar

2 cups boiling water

Steep tea bags in boiling water. Pour into a tea pitcher.
Stir in sugar. Add cold water to fill pitcher.

Yield: 12 servings

Sunshine Punch

Refreshing. For a kick, add champagne.

1 (6-ounce) can frozen orange juice concentrate, thawed

1 (6-ounce) can frozen lemonade, thawed

1 (6-ounce) can frozen limeade, thawed

4 cups cold water

1 quart lemon-lime carbonated beverage, chilled

Blend orange juice, lemonade, limeade, water and carbonated beverage. Mix well and refrigerate.

Yield: 20 servings

Decorative Ice Cubes:
Make ice cubes festive for a party by freezing sprigs of mint, maraschino cherries, lemon or orange peel in them.

Lemonade Mojitos

Get your party started with this variation of a traditional Cuban cocktail.

- SIMPLE SYRUP -

1 cup sugar   1 cup water

Heat sugar and water over low heat, stirring with a wooden spoon until sugar dissolves. Stop stirring and increase to medium heat. Simmer 2 minutes. Remove from heat and cool. Refrigerate 2 hours before using.

- LEMONADE MIX -

½ cup mint leaves   ⅔ cup super fine sugar

5 cups club soda   lemon rounds and mint sprigs

4 cups vodka   for garnish

4 cups fresh lemon juice

In a large bowl, mash mint leaves with simple syrup. Stir in club soda, vodka, lemon juice and sugar. Refrigerate. Pour into pitchers with lemon rounds and mint sprigs.

Yield: 20 servings

Heat lemons or limes in a microwave oven for a few seconds. The lemons give much more juice when warmed. Roll them with the palm of your hand with slight pressure before cutting to juice.

Liquid Gold

Champagne is always a great celebration beverage.
Try this interesting combination at your next special event.

1 fresh pineapple, peeled and cored   1 (750 ml) bottle dry champagne

Purée the flesh of pineapple in a blender.
Combine with champagne in a chilled pitcher.

Yield: 6 to 8 servings

Pear Martinis with Lemon and Rosemary

Flavored martinis are all the hit. Try this Pear Martini.

- SIMPLE SYRUP -

1 cup sugar   4 (3-inch) rosemary sprigs

1 cup water

Bring sugar and water to boil in small pan. Stir until sugar dissolves.
Add rosemary. Reduce heat and simmer 10 minutes.
Discard rosemary and cool.

- MARTINI MIX -

1 (750 ml) bottle good vodka   12 ice cubes

5 tablespoons fresh lemon juice   12 small rosemary sprigs

¼ cup pear brandy

Mix syrup with the vodka, juice and brandy in a large pitcher.
Place in freezer 3 hours until cold. Remove from pitcher
and stir in ice cubes. Strain mixture into chilled glasses.
Garnish each glass with small rosemary sprig.

Yield: 12 servings

Fabulous Cosmopolitan Cocktail

If you prefer a less sweet cosmopolitan, use cranberry juice instead
of cranberry/raspberry cocktail. Replace the Roses sweetened lime juice
with real lime juice and use nonflavored vodka.

7 parts cranberry/raspberry juice cocktail	2 parts Triple Sec
1 part Roses sweetened lime juice	4 parts Stoli or Smirnoff raspberry vodka
1 part Chambord	1 splash Cointreau

Measure ingredients by utilizing a shot glass or the top of your martini
shaker. Pour ingredients into a pitcher with ice or a martini shaker with ice.
Stir or shake approximately 1 minute. Strain mixture into four martini glasses.

Yield: 4 servings

Holiday Eggnog

There is nothing better than fresh homemade eggnog.

6 large eggs	1 cup white rum
1 cup sugar	1 quart half-and-half
½ teaspoon salt	fresh ground nutmeg

Beat eggs with an electric mixer 5 minutes until foamy.
Gradually add sugar until well blended. Add salt. Beat on medium
speed until mixture is lemon colored. Stir in rum and half-and-half.
Refrigerate at least 3 hours before serving. Serve from a pitcher
or punch bowl in small glasses. Sprinkle with nutmeg.

Yield: 15 servings

Bourbon Slush

This beverage is a hit for large gatherings and can be
served year-round. Great for holiday celebrations, festive occasions
and especially Kentucky Derby parties! Mixture can be made 3 to 4 days
ahead and frozen in a large container. Stir every 6 to 8 hours
to keep the mixture loose and evenly frozen.

2 cups hot strong tea, 4 tea bags
steeped in 2 cups boiling water

1 cup sugar

2 (6-ounce) cans frozen lemonade

1 (6-ounce) can frozen
orange juice

5 cups crushed ice

2 cups ice water

2 cups bourbon

1 quart cold ginger ale

mint sprigs for garnish

At least 6 hours before serving, combine tea and sugar in a 1 gallon
plastic or glass container. Stir until dissolved. Add lemonade and juice and
stir until thawed. In a blender, in batches, blend ice with enough of the ice
water to make a slush. Add to tea mixture. Add remaining ice water. Stir in
bourbon. If ice will not purée, blend in bourbon instead of water. Add water
later. Pour slush into several shallow plastic containers. Freeze until ready
to serve. Break up slush by stirring about every 2 hours, allowing mixture to
freeze evenly. To serve, spoon slush into tall or stemmed glasses
and top off with ginger ale. Garnish with a sprig of mint.

Yield: 16 servings

Fresh and Spicy Bloody Mary's

3 pounds tomatoes (heirloom if possible), cored and coarsely cut

2 to 3 jalapeño peppers, stems removed and coarsely cut

1 fennel bulb, white part coarsely cut

salt and pepper to taste

3 tablespoons Worcestershire sauce

1 tablespoon extra-virgin olive oil

1 lemon, halved

½ cup favorite spice rub

6 to 8 whole red jalapeños peppers

lemon vodka

Combine tomatoes, jalapeños and fennel in a bowl. Season liberally with salt and pepper. Stir in Worcestershire sauce. Add oil and toss to lightly coat. Purée a few tomatoes in a blender. Add the remaining tomato mixture to blender. Process until liquefied. Refrigerate up to 6 hours. To serve, rub a cut lemon around the rim of a chilled martini glass. Dip glass into salt or spice rub. Slice the tip of a red jalapeño and slide over the glass rim. Pour Bloody Mary mixture into glass. Add 1 ounce vodka. Stir carefully and serve.

Yield: 6 to 8 servings

The celery stick met the Bloody Mary in the 1960s at Chicago's Ambassador East Hotel. Legend has it that an unnamed celebrity got a Bloody Mary, but no swizzle stick. So, he grabbed a stalk of celery from the relish tray to stir his Bloody Mary.

The Junior League of Evanston-North Shore would like to thank the members of the League whose contributions of wonderful recipes, diligent testing and commitment to excellence lead to the creation of this book.

Recipe and Testing Contributors:

Alissa Preston
Amy Bennett
Amy Findlay
Amy Maher
Ann Hartman
Beth Kauffman
Betsy Flanagan
Cathy Tobben Schulte
Cindy Dooley
Deborah Gale
Diane Nekritz
Elizabeth Thomas
Erica Smith
Frances Hopps
Guion Stewart-Moore
Heather Burgess
Jane Lahey

Jeannine James
Jennifer Edstrom
Julia R. Johnson
Karen Cosgrove
Karen Miller
Kathy Cullerton
Kathryn Talty
Kelly Kraklau Bosker
Kristin K. Mehigan
LeAnita Ragland-Brooks
Leesa Ullerich
Lisa Morgensai
Marian Baird
Marley Crane
Mary Hagene
Mary Walther
Megan McAleer

Nancy Free
Nell Pike
Nicole Bogdanovich
Nina Gray
Pam Kerr
Penny Green
Rebecca Garces
Rikki Ragland-Marver
Rita Brogley
Sarah Condry
Stephanie Wilson
Sue Laue
Susan Boatman
Garland
Tammy Gibbons
Theresa Gernand
Zoe T. Barron

Thank you to the following members of our community for their support:

Alinea

Books on Vernon

Cajun Charlie's New Orleans Kitchen

Charlie Trotters

Coldwater Creek

Corner Cooks

Crystal Cave

Eggymeyer and Graham Orthodontia

Gabriels Restaurant

Great Harvest Bread Company

Mille de Fleur

Oceanique

Old Willow Wine Shoppe

Potocki Vodka

Rosie Toys

Schaefer's Wines, Foods and Spirits

Song O'Sixpence

The Bookstall

Three Tarts Bakery and Catering

Walter E. Smithe Custom Furniture

Index

A

B

**JUNIOR LEAGUE OF
EVANSTON-NORTH SHORE**
Women building better communities

It's A Shore Thing...

Culinary Favorites from Chicago's North Shore

Cookbook Order Form

To order more books, please complete the below form and either phone, fax or mail your order to the Junior League of Evanston-North Shore (JLE-NS).

Name: _____

Address: _____

Phone: _____ E-mail: _____

Book Retail Price = $24.95 each

Tax = 7.75% $1.93 each (Illinois residents only)

Shipping and handling = $5.00 each

Accepted methods of payment -
Cash, Check, Visa and MasterCard (please do not send cash)

Checks should be made out to the
Junior League of Evanston-North Shore (JLE-NS).

Visa or MasterCard # _____

Expiration Date: _____

Name on Card (please print): _____

Signature: _____

Proceeds: The Junior League of Evanston-North Shore is an organization of women, committed to promoting volunteerism, developing the potential of women, and improving the community through the effective action and leadership of trained volunteers. Its purpose is exclusively educational and charitable. Proceeds from the sale of *It's a Shore Thing... Culinary Favorites from Chicago's North Shore* will support the projects and programs of the JLE-NS.

Junior League of Evanston-North Shore
Cookbook Committee
614 Lincoln Ave.
Winnetka, IL 60093

Phone: (847)441-0995
Fax: (847)441-6423

For more information, please visit our website at www.jle-ns.org